Identification & Pr

Winnie the Pooh

Collectibles **II**

by Carol J. Smith

Published by  Hobby House Press, Inc.
Grantsville, Maryland 21536

ACKNOWLEDGMENTS

I'd like to thank Dave Smith at the Walt Disney Archives for his assistance with information regarding manufacturers and dates. I'd also like to thank Marc Anderson who contributed directly to this book by sharing a rare item from his collection, and Debbie Gibbins from England and Gina Uccelatore from Belgium for trading numerous European Poohs for American Poohs and Disneyana, therefore, augmenting the European items featured in this book. Lastly, a special thank you to Mary Beth Ruddell of Hobby House Press for her wonderful job making this book a reality.

Winnie the Pooh Collectibles II is an independent study by the author Carol J. Smith and published by Hobby House Press, Inc. The research and publication of this book were not sponsored in any way by the manufacturers of the dolls, the doll costumes, and the doll accessories featured in this study. Photographs of the collectibles were from dolls, costumes, or accessories belonging to Carol J. Smith at the time the picture was taken unless otherwise credited with the caption.

The information as to the ownership pertains to documentary materials contemporary with the doll or doll's accessories. Ownership of the registered trademark, the trademark, or the copyright may have expired or been transferred to another owner.

The values given within this book are intended as value guides rather than arbitrarily set prices. The values quoted are as accurate as possible but in the case of errors, typographical, clerical or otherwise, the author and publisher assume no liability nor responsibility for any loss incurred by users of this book.

This book makes references to various DISNEY® Winnie the Pooh characters. The copyrights to these characters are owned by Disney Enterprises, Inc.

Additional copies of this book may be purchased at $14.95 (plus postage and handling) from

Hobby House Press, Inc.
1 Corporate Drive
Grantsville, Maryland 21536
1-800-554-1447
or from your favorite bookstore or dealer.

©1996 Carol J. Smith

Printed in the United States of America.

ISBN: 0-87588-466-0

TABLE
OF
CONTENTS

INTRODUCTION

When developing the first *Identification & Price Guide to Winnie the Pooh Collectibles*, it became obvious that I would only be able to include a small fraction of the items found on the collectibles market. Hence, this second book was developed to cover some common sought-after items that were not mentioned at all in the first book. These items include watches, clocks, toys, and lamps. This second book also identifies plush, ceramic figurines, and Christmas items that are on the collectibles market, but were not included in the first guide due to scarcity or recent development.

On the collectibles market, the condition of the item greatly influences the price. In this guide, the condition of the item in the photograph is listed prior to each price estimate. I attempted to choose conditions that were commonly reflective of the item in the market, at least in a form that is still considered desirable by collectors. Rare, old, and foreign items are difficult to obtain, and their condition is often less than pristine. Unless otherwise stated, the price estimate of each item assumes that the item is in its original state and possesses all clothing and accessories except the original packaging. If an item has been altered, such as the replacement of eyes or clothing on a plush character, than the listed value should be significantly decreased. Because the value is dependent on the maintenance of original parts, I tried to describe each item in detail with particular attention to potentially replaceable parts, such as eyes, noses, and clothing. This will hopefully provide you with a better price estimate of the item that you are trying to identify.

For identification and dating references, information was obtained through Sears catalogs from the mid-1960s to the early 1990s, Disney Catalogs, manufacturers' brochures, and personal observations, as well as the knowledge of other collectors. I also visited the Disney Archives to research items that were difficult to accurately date.

The approximate size of most items is provided. Unless otherwise stated, the measurements are from the top of the head to the tip of the toes. Eeyore is often measured in this manner as well as lengthwise (from the tip of his nose to the end of his seat). My measurements do not include the length of upright long ears (such as Rabbit's). Please view the measurements as approximations, within an inch in each direction, because of the variations in manufacturing and measuring.

The toy chapter reviews commonly found Pooh toys on the market, yet still only represents a small portion of what is available I tried to choose many of the toys that I have seen in collectible periodicals and at toy shows and antique stores, but this chapter covers highlights and is not an exhaustive review for these items.

The price estimates are based upon observations and purchases at toy shows, antique and collectibles stores and shows on the west coast, and through publications that advertise collectibles. The publications are distributed internationally and reflect a broad market sector, with particular distribution throughout the United States. Price estimates are relative to the U.S. market. Items from Japan and Europe might be less expensive in their country of origin than in the United States. Similarly, U.S. items might be more expensive in foreign countries than here.

When developing your Pooh collection, it is advisable to contact other Pooh collectors. You can help each other find items for your collections. Often, another Pooh collector will specialize in certain types of items, such as items of Pooh and not the other characters, or only plush and watches. They can find either duplicate items for you or items that are in your area of interest but not in theirs. The additional contacts are useful as price checks as well. It is common for Pooh collectors to readily share information about the items and prices seen at shows and antique stores. I can happily state that nearly all of the Pooh collectors I have met have been wonderful people who have enriched my life. And, we usually find that we have many other things in common. As my collection of Pooh grows, so does my collection of friends. So, have fun with your Pooh collections! Happy hunting and happy sharing.

1. Carol Stewart, circa 1991. This limited edition (100 pieces) Pooh sold at the 1991 Walt Disney World Teddy Bear Convention. Made of shimmering yellow velvet, Pooh is fully jointed and wears a red cloth shirt. He has black beaded eyes and a black threaded nose and mouth. 6in (15cm). Mint condition in original clear plastic box: **$350-450**.

2. Chad Valley, circa 1940s. The jointed mohair Pooh has amber and black glass eyes and a black threaded mouth and nose. He wears a red felt shirt fastened by a single white button. 6-1/4in (16cm). Excellent condition: **$450-550**.

4. Determined Productions Inc., circa 1963. *Left:* The Piglet hand puppet has a black and white striped cotton body, pink felt arms, stuffed head, black plastic bead eyes, and a red felt tie around the neck. The pink paper tag reads, "This is Piglet 'Friend of Pooh Bear'", "Copyright @ Stephen Slesinger". Slesinger owned the rights to the Pooh characters prior to The Walt Disney Company. 9in (23cm). Near mint condition: **$175-250**. *Right:* The brown felt Pooh has a red removable cloth shirt, black plastic bead eyes, and black cloth nose. The pink paper tag reads "This is Winnie the Pooh". 12in (31cm). Near mint condition: **$175-250**.

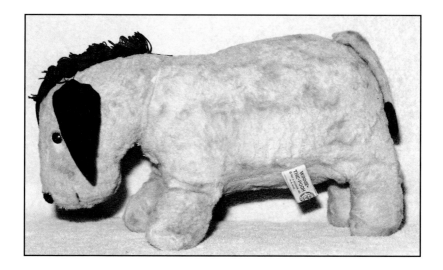

5. Knickerbocker Toy Company, Inc., circa 1963. The gray plush Eeyore has a black yarn mane and tail tip, black felt ears, two black pom-pom nostrils, a black threaded mouth, and black plastic eyes on a white felt background. His legs are reinforced with wire. He is tagged "Winnie-The-Pooh 1963 S. Slesinger, Inc. A.A. Milne." 13in (33cm) long, 8in (20cm) tall. Very good condition: **$150-200**.

Previous Page: 3. Agnes Brush, circa 1940s-1950s. *Left:* Rabbit is covered with tan felt and has a white tail, underside and inside of ears. His eyes are printed in black, and his whiskers consist of white threads. 11in (28cm). Near mint condition: **$350-450**. *Right:* Eeyore is covered with gray felt, accented with black yarn for his mane and tail tip. His eyes and mouth are denoted by a single line of black thread. Snaps secure the removable tail. 7in (18cm) high, 12in (31cm) long. Near mint condition: **$350-450**.

6. Gund Mfg. Co., circa 1964. The tan plush Poohs have yellow removable shirts trimmed with red and white stripes. Black "Winnie the Pooh" letters are printed on the front of the shirts. Each Pooh has a red stocking hat, glass two-toned eyes, and a red felt mouth. One of the most unique characteristics are the bottoms of their feet, which are printed with "paw prints". Two versions include an 11in (28cm) standing Pooh (left) and a 9in (23cm) sitting Pooh (right). Excellent condition: **$200-275**.

7. Walt Disney Productions, circa mid-to-late 1960s. This gold plush Pooh has a bell in one ear, black plastic eyes, a small black pom-pom nose, and a red felt mouth. Pooh wears a red bib trimmed in white printed with white "Pooh" letters. 11in (28cm). Near mint condition: **$45-60**.

8. Gund Mfg. Co., circa 1964-1968. The gold plush talking Pooh has a red cotton shirt with yellow "Pooh" letters embroidered on the front of the shirt, black plastic eyes, and a black pom-pom nose. Each pull of the string plays part of a 12-line poem, in the following order: "I'm filled with fluff."; "When I run, I huff and puff."; "I speak in rhymes."; "I play all the time"; "I feel funny in honey."; "Honey tastes good. Yummy"; "Eeyore, Kanga and Baby Roo"; "Piglet and Tigger too"; "Live in the land of Pooh"; "I love you."; "Winnie the Pooh"; "Wish you could be here too"; "We love you and you." This talking version is less common than the one produced by Gund in the 1970s. 14in (36cm). Excellent condition: **$125-175**.

9. *Left:* Gund Mfg. Co., circa 1964-1968. The gold plush Pooh has a red cotton removable shirt and a wind-up mechanism in his back that moves Pooh's head side-to-side while the Winnie the Pooh theme plays. He has black plastic eyes, a black pom-pom nose, and a red felt mouth. 9in (23cm). Very good condition: **$100-150.** *Right:* Gund Mfg. Co., circa 1964-1968. The gold plush reclining Pooh was sold by Sears. This piece is missing the original red cape. Pooh has black plastic eyes, a black pom-pom nose, and a red felt mouth. 9in (23cm) long. Very good condition: **$55-70** with cape; **$25-35** without cape.

10. Gund Mfg. Co., circa 1966-1968. *Left:* The peach corduroy covered Roo is woodchip-filled, and has a blue shirt, red felt mouth, brown felt nose, black vinyl eyes, while his eyebrows are printed in black. 6in (15cm). Center: The yellow and black striped Heffalump has white gauze wings shaped with wire, a black tail, black felt eyebrows, black and white felt eyes, and a black printed mouth. 5in (13cm) long, not including trunk. *Right:* The yellow corduroy Rabbit is woodchip-filled and is accented with a white belly and muzzle. His ear linings are pink; his eyes are white with black pupils and peach lids; his nose is brown felt. His eyebrows and mouth are threaded in black, and he has black plastic whiskers. His arms are floppy, and he has a white fluffy tail. 6in (15cm) tall. All of these versions are very rare and command a higher price than the more common woodchip-filled Pooh characters. Very good condition: **$65-85** each.

11. Gund Mfg. Co., circa mid-1960s. *Left:* Standing brown plush Rabbit has wire-reinforced pink rayon ear linings, white plush muzzle, tail and belly, amber and black plastic eyes (same style as Gopher's, [see page 11]) on a black felt background, black pom-pom nose, white threaded whiskers, red felt mouth, and pink felt feet bottoms. Tag also reads "Winnie The Pooh". 12in (30cm) excluding ears. Near mint condition: **$125-175**. *Right:* Standing pink plush Piglet has wire-reinforced legs, pink felt ears and feet bottoms, black button eyes, a black felt mouth, and pink and white checked sewn-in shirt. 9in (23cm) tall excluding ears. Excellent condition: **$85-100**.

12. Sears, circa 1976. The Eeyore hobby horse has a gray stuffed head mounted on a stick. Eeyore has a blue muzzle and ear linings, black felt eyebrows, nostrils and mouth, black and white paper eyes, and yarn reins. 37in (94cm) overall height. Very good condition: **$95-125**.

13. Gund Mfg. Co., circa mid-1960s. The foam-filled plush Heffalump is yellow with black stripes and has gauze wings outlined with a canvas-type of material. He has white and black plastic eyes, black cloth eyebrows, and black antenna. Wire supports the wings, ears, and front legs. The tag reads: "Walt Disney Character" instead of the usual inscription of "Winnie the Pooh". *From the collection of Marc Anderson. Photo courtesy of Marc Anderson.* 12in long (30cm) Near mint condition: **$150-175**.

14. Gund Mfg. Co., circa mid-1960s. *Left:* Standing tan plush Pooh has wire-reinforced legs, black button eyes, and a black pom-pom nose. He is wearing a blue shirt trimmed in red and white labeled "Winnie The-Pooh. The blue shirt is very uncommon for Gund Poohs. 14in (35cm). Excellent condition: **$100-125**. *Right:* Standing brown plush Gopher has reinforced black felt feet, black felt hands, tail and ears, blue and black plastic eyes on a black felt background, black pom-pom nose, black threaded whiskers, two white felt teeth, a white plush muzzle, and tan plush belly. 11in (28cm). Near mint condition: **$125-175**.

15. Sears, circa 1976. Plush gray Eeyore slipper holder with blue plush muzzle, black and white paper eyes, black felt mane, nostrils and mouth. 5-1/2in (14cm) wide, 7in (18cm) high. Good condition: **$30-40**.

16. Commonwealth Toy & Novelty Co. Inc., circa 1970s. The Pooh footstool's back and head are gold plush, while the sides and bottom are red. Pooh has black plastic eyes, black felt eyebrows, a black pom-pom nose, and a red felt mouth. A yellow ribbon printed "Winnie the Pooh" is sewn into the stool. This item was sold through Sears. 9in (23cm) high, 18in (46cm) long. Very good condition: **$50-75**.

17. *Left:* Gund, circa 1992-1993. This yellow and red terry cloth Pooh squeaks when squeezed. Pooh has black threaded eyebrows and eyes, a black terry cloth nose, and a red threaded mouth. The red sewn-in shirt has yellow "Pooh" lettering across the chest. This was sold through Sears in a decorative Pooh bag. 7in (18cm). Mint condition: **$25-35**. *Right:* Canasa Trading Co, circa 1992. The gold plush Grad Night '92 Pooh is a non-jointed special edition Pooh sold at the Disney Parks to graduating seniors at a special event. Pooh has black threaded eyebrows, black plastic eyes, a black cloth nose, and a red cloth mouth. Pooh is wearing a black felt-covered mortar board with a gold tassel and a red removable shirt decorated with white "Pooh" lettering. 8in (20cm). Mint condition: **$35-50**.

18. Walt Disney Productions, circa early to mid-1980s. *Left:* The yellow Pooh is wearing a red velvet shirt with white "Pooh" letters printed on the front. This Pooh has black felt eyebrows and eyes, a black pom-pom nose, and a black threaded mouth. His head is plush, but his ears and body are cloth covered. 6in (15cm). Near mint condition: **$30-40**. *Right:* The 7in (18cm) yellow plush Pooh is wearing a red plush sewn-in shirt, and has black felt eyebrows and eyes, a black cloth-covered hard nose, and a black threaded mouth. Excellent condition: **$20-30**.

19. The Walt Disney Company, circa 1994. The gold plush Pooh is wearing a red knit sweater and scarf, both trimmed in gold, red ear muffs, black vinyl skates on black cloth feet. His facial features include black threaded eyebrows, black plastic eyes, a red cloth mouth, and black cloth nose. Pooh's bottom is mounted on a black plastic base that revolves and plays the "Winnie the Pooh" theme when wound. This plush was sold at The Disney Store for a very short time. 10in (25cm). Mint condition. **$65-85.**

20. *Left:* Canasa Trading Corp., circa 1993. A tangerine plush Pooh is attired for Christmas with a green and red plaid shirt and red stocking hat embroidered with yellow "Pooh" Letters. Pooh is holding a gold foil wrapped gift with red ribbon and white tag. His facial features are black threaded eyebrows, black plastic eyes, a brown nose, and red mouth. 11in (28cm). Mint condition: **$45-60.** *Right:* Euro Disneyland, circa 1994. This plush Pooh is similar to the U.S. version, but differs in the following ways: the color is yellow, and his shirt is a slightly different plaid design; plaid decorates Pooh's bottom paw pads; and the European Pooh plays "Jingle Bells" when his paw is pressed. 11in (28cm). Mint condition: **$65-75.**

21. The Walt Disney Company (England), circa 1994. This 14in (36cm) tangerine plush Pooh was sold at The Disney Store in London. Pooh is wearing a red shirt decorated with yellow letters spelling "Pooh", a green and red scarf, and a red hat with a white pom-pom. He is holding a red and green plaid cloth box containing a 5-1/2in (14cm) pink plush Piglet. Piglet has a purple and black striped shirt sewn into his body. Mint condition: **$75-100**.

22. Walt Disney Productions, circa early to mid-1980s. *Left:* The 10in (25cm) yellow plush Pooh is wearing a red velvet removable shirt closed with Velcro. Pooh has black felt eyebrows and eyes, a black pom-pom nose, and a black threaded mouth. Excellent condition: **$25-35**. *Right:* The 8in (20cm) yellow plush Pooh has the same features as the 10in (25cm) version. Excellent condition: **$20-30**.

14

23. Walt Disney Productions, circa 1990. *Left:* The blue-gray plush Eeyore has a light gray underside, muzzle and tail, a black hairy mane and tail tip, black and white plastic eyes, black threaded nostrils, and pink inside of his ears. 7-1/2in (19cm) long. *Center:* The 6in (15cm) yellow plush Pooh is wearing a red shirt and white "Pooh" lettering on the front. He has black plastic eyes and nose and a black threaded mouth. *Right:* The orange and black striped Tigger has a yellow belly, muzzle, eye area, and inside of ears. Tigger has black plastic eyes, a brown plastic nose, and a brown cloth mouth. 6-1/2in (16cm) tall. Each of these were available only at the Disney Store. Mint condition: **$20-30** each.

24. Mattel, Inc., circa 1994. These plush figures were sold in England and differ from the versions sold in the United States. *Left:* 9in (23cm) yellow Pooh is standing and wearing a red shirt with white "Pooh" letters on the front. He has a red cloth mouth, black plastic nose, black plastic eyes, and black threaded eyebrows. *Center:* 8in(20cm) sitting Tigger is orange with black stripes and a white belly, muzzle, ear and eye linings. Tigger has black plastic eyes, black threaded eyebrows, a brown cloth nose, and pink cloth mouth. *Right:* 8in (20cm) Piglet is peach with a pink and red striped sewn-in shirt. He has a flesh colored cloth nose, black plastic eyes, black threaded eyebrows and mouth. Mint condition: **$35-45** each.

25. Euro Disneyland, circa 1992. These plush dolls are identical to those sold in the U.S., but the sewn-in tags read "EuroDisney" and the hanging paper tags list the name of the characters in French. *Left to right:* The brown and pink plush Kanga (Grand Gourou) has a black plastic nose and eyes, a black threaded mouth and eyebrows, and black cloth eyelashes. 16in (41cm). Mint condition: **$50**. The brown plush 9in (23cm) Roo (Petit Gourou) is wearing a blue shirt. Roo has a black plastic nose and eyes, pink ear linings, and a brown tuft of hair. Mint condition: **$35-45**. The 9in (23cm) orange and black striped Tigger (Tigrou) has a yellow muzzle and belly, black plastic eyes, a brown cloth nose and mouth, and brown plush paw pads. Mint condition: **$40-50**. The gray and white plush sitting Eeyore (Boursiquet) has black and white plastic eyes, black threaded nostrils and eyebrows, and a black furry mane and tail tip. 8in (20cm). Mint condition: **$35-45**. The pink plush Piglet (Porcinet) is constructed with a sewn-in purple and black striped shirt, and has black plastic eyes, black threaded eyebrows and mouth, and a pink plush nose. 7in (18cm). Mint condition: **$30-40**. The yellow non-jointed plush Pooh (Winnie L'Ourson) is wearing a red velveteen shirt decorated with white "Pooh" lettering. He has black plastic eyes, a black cloth covered nose, black threaded eyebrows, and a red cloth mouth. 14in (36cm). Mint condition: **$50-60**.

Opposite Page: 27. Left: R. John Wright Dolls, circa 1993. The limited edition (3500 pieces) tan mohair Pooh is wearing a rust felt vest. Pooh is fully jointed and has black glass beaded eyes and black threaded nose and mouth. 5in (13cm) standing. He comes with a small booklet containing E.H. Shepard illustrations and Pooh literature verses regarding Pooh. Mint condition in original box: **$550-650**. *Right:* R. John Wright Dolls, circa 1994. Fully-jointed pink wool felt Piglet has a green shirt with tiny buttons down the front, black glass beaded eyes and dark pink blush. 2-1/2in (4cm) standing. He comes with a small booklet containing E.H. Shepard illustrations and Pooh literature verses regarding Piglet. Limited edition of 3500. Mint condition in original box: **$250** and likely to increase after the edition sells out.

26. R. John Wright Dolls, circa 1994. This special edition of Wintertime Pooh and Piglet was limited to 250 pieces, and sold only through FAO Schwarz in New York. The fully-jointed tan mohair Pooh is wearing a felt maroon vest and a gray scarf. Pooh has black glass beaded eyes and a black threaded nose and mouth. 5in (13cm) standing. The fully-jointed pink wool felt-covered Piglet is wearing a green shirt with small pearl buttons down the front and a red scarf. He has black glass beaded eyes and dark pink blush. 2-1/2in (4cm) standing. They were sold as a set and accompany a small booklet containing E.H. Shepard illustrations and Pooh literature verses. Mint condition in original box: **$950-1,200**.

28. *Left:* Robin Woods, circa 1983. This doll features Christopher Robin, and is called "Vespers" after a poem written by A. A. Milne. The poem is printed on a paper tag that is attached to the doll. Christopher's body is cloth, rag-doll style, and his face is painted hard cloth. He has light brown hair and blue eyes, and is wearing a blue robe with attached hood, over a white cotton body suit. Three plastic tiny angels serve as buttons on the robe. 20in (51cm). Mint condition: **$175-250**. *Right:* Robin Woods, circa 1990. A later version of the Vespers doll is constructed of vinyl. Christopher Robin is wearing a blue flannel robe trimmed with blue ducks. The robe covers blue and white striped pajamas. Christopher is also wearing white underpants and blue vinyl slippers that are decorated with small blue pom-poms. He has light brown hair and blue eyes, and is carrying a blue blanket and a white pillow. The pillow is adorned with a blue duck appliqué. This later version did not include a copy of A. A. Milne's Vespers poem. 8in (20cm). Mint condition in original box: **$60-75**.

30. Sears (Canada), circa 1980s. Pooh is covered with yellow deep-pile plush and has black plastic button eyes. He is wearing a red polyester shirt inked with yellow "Pooh" letters. 22in (55cm). Excellent condition: **$60-80**.

31. Sears, circa early 1970s. The yellow and red plush Pooh slipper holder has black cloth eyebrows, black plastic eyes, a black pom-pom nose, and a red plush pocket to hold slippers. 15in (38cm). Very good condition: **$25-35**. Sears, circa 1980s. The tan plush Pooh slippers have red cloth shirts, black plastic eyes, black threaded eyebrows and mouth. Very good condition: **$15-25**.

Previous Page: **29.** Commonwealth Toy & Novelty Co., Inc., circa 1981-1982. The yellow plush reclining Pooh pajama bag is wearing a red shirt with yellow "Pooh" lettering. Pooh has a red felt mouth, black plastic eyes, a black pom-pom nose, and a zipper in his tummy. 20in (51cm). Near mint condition: **$40-50**.

32. Marks & Spencer (England), circa 1987. This honey-colored plush Pooh hand puppet is wearing a red shirt with an appliqué of a bee flying near white embroidered "Pooh" lettering. Pooh has brown felt eyebrows, eyes, and nose, and a black threaded mouth. Near mint condition: **$55-75**.

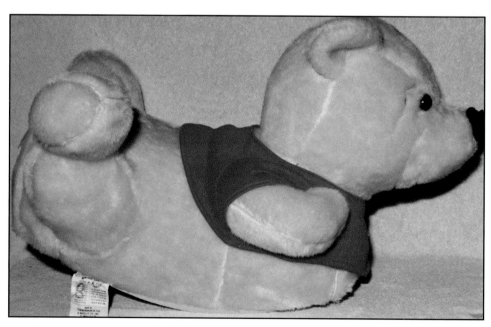

33. Commonwealth Toy and Novelty Co, circa 1988. The yellow plush Pooh rocker is mounted on a curved wooden base. Pooh is wearing a red polyester shirt, and has black threaded eyebrows and mouth, black plastic eyes, and a black pom-pom nose. 23in (58cm) long, 18in (46cm) high. Mint condition: **$100-125**.

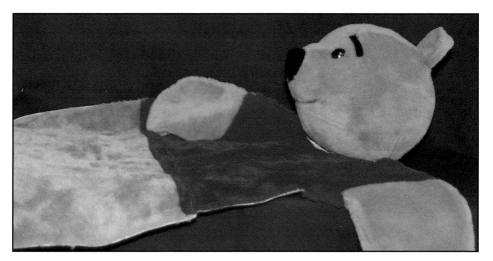

34. Sears, circa 1988. The brown plush Pooh rug has a red plush shirt sewn into the rug. Pooh's head is stuffed, and accented with black plush eyebrows, black plastic eyes, a black pom-pom nose, and a red cloth mouth. 44in (116cm) long. Mint condition: **$85-100**.

35. John Adams Toy Company (England), circa mid-1980s. *Left:* The plush 18in (46cm) pale yellow Pooh is wearing a red felt shirt, has amber and black plastic eyes, a black threaded nose and mouth. Mint condition: **$175-225**. *Center:* 11in (28cm) Piglet has black threaded eyes and a dark green cor-duroy sewn-in shirt. He can be found in either pink cotton or pink felt versions. Mint condition: **$100-150**. *Right:* 11in (28cm) Owl is covered in a long-pile plush of white, gray, and black. Peach felt is used for Owl's feet and beak, while his plastic eyes are amber and black. Mint condition: **$200-250**.

21

36. John Adams Toy Company (England), circa mid-1980s. Set of "Sew Your Own" kits of Piglet (4in [10cm]), Tigger (6in [15cm]), Eeyore (4in [10cm]) and Pooh (5in [13cm]). Each kit includes cut cloth, accessories and instructions. Piglet is made from pink felt and a green cloth body. Tigger is made from a tan and black striped plush. Eeyore consists of gray felt, and Pooh is made from a tan plush and has a red shirt. Mint in original box: **$50-75** each.

37. John Adams Toy Company (England), circa mid-1980s. The plush 15in (38cm) brown and tan Kanga accompanies 7in (18cm) Roo. Kanga has amber and black plastic eyes and a black threaded nose and mouth. Roo has brown threaded eyes; his other facial features are undefined. He can be fully removed from Kanga's pocket. Mint condition: **$200-250**.

38. John Adams Toy Company (England), circa mid-1980s. The 4-1/2 (11cm) tall, 7-1/2in (19cm) long, dark gray plush Eeyore has light gray felt ears, black and white felt eyes, a black felt mane and tail tip. Mint condition: **$50-75**. (Flowers not included)

39. Sears, circa 1976-1977. The Pooh slipper bag consists of a gold plush head and a red cotton shirt with pockets for slippers. Pooh has black felt eyebrows, eyes, nose and mouth, in addition to a red felt tongue. 18in (46cm) tall. Very good condition. **$25-35**. Sears, circa 1981-1983. The Pooh slippers have red plush bodies, yellow stretch fabric at the ankles, and gold plastic heads. Atop the heads are red and white striped stocking hats. Very good condition: **$15-20**.

40. Sears, circa 1988-1989. The yellow plush 16in (41cm) Pooh nursery monitor is wearing a removable red velveteen shirt with yellow "Pooh" lettering. Pooh has black plastic eyes, black threaded eyebrows, a black pom-pom nose, a movable pink mouth, and a zipper in back that opens the battery compartment. Pooh came with a walkie-talkie unit so that when Pooh was left in baby's room, the parent could talk to the baby through the walkie-talkie. Pooh's mouth would move as the parent's voice could be heard. Tagged TCA Group Inc. Mint condition with original walkie-talkie: **$125-150**. Excellent condition without walkie-talkie: **$30-45**.

41. Marks & Spencer (England), circa 1989. *Left:* This yellow plush Pooh is wearing a red shirt with yellow embroidered "Pooh" lettering and a small bee appliqué near the lettering. Pooh has a red mouth, black plastic eyes, and black velvet nose. 11in (28cm). Excellent condition: **$55-75**. *Right:* The plush tan slippers have red felt trim for shirts with two yellow felt "buttons". Stuffed heads are mounted on the front of the slippers and have brown cloth facial features. Excellent condition: **$30-40**.

42. Sears Canada Inc, circa late 1980s-early 1990s. The gray plush Eeyore has a white muzzle and underside, pink cloth ear linings, black threaded eyebrows and nostrils, black furry mane and tail tip, and black and white plastic eyes. The eyes look sideways; a characteristic that is uncommon for Eeyore. 6in (15cm). Near mint condition: **$35-45**.

44. John Adams Toy Company (England), circa mid-1980s. Dark gray Eeyore has light gray inside of his ears and a black felt mane and tail tip. His eyes are amber and plastic, and his nostrils and mouth are threaded in black. Flaps of plush are sewn over Eeyore's eyes to create heavy eyebrows. Eeyore's tail attaches with Velcro. 9in (23cm) tall, 14in (36cm) long. Mint condition: **$200-250**.

45. John Adams Toy Company (England), circa mid-1980s. *Left:* 5in (13cm) tan plush Pooh is wearing a red cloth shirt and has black threaded features. Mint condition: **$50-75**. *Right:* The 6in (15cm) tan and black plush Tigger has a black felt nose and black and yellow felt eyes. Mint condition: **$50-75**.

Opposite Page: **43.** *Left:* Anne Wilkinson Designs Ltd. (England), circa 1986-1989. This yellow and black striped stuffed 14in (36cm) Tigger has a white belly and printed facial features on quilted fabric. The quilted design does not extend to the belly. Mint condition: **$100-125**. *Right:* Anne Wilkinson Designs Ltd. (England), circa 1990s. The newer version of Tigger is orange with black stripes accented with white ear linings and belly. The quilted design covers all of Tigger. His facial features are painted onto the fabric. 14in (36cm). Mint condition **$50-65**.

46. The Boots Company (England), circa early 1990s. The plush tan Pooh hot water bottle cover has an acrylic red shirt, black plastic eyes, and black threaded eyebrows, nose, and mouth. 16in (41cm). Mint in package: **$50-75**.

47. Gund, Inc., circa 1992-1995. *Left to right:* The orange and brown striped plush Baby Tigger has a tan belly, cream muzzle, pink plush nose, black plastic eyes, red cloth mouth, and black plastic whiskers. The light tan plush Baby Piglet has a pink plush striped body, pink striped hat, black plastic eyes, a pink cloth nose, and a red cloth mouth. The gray plush Baby Eeyore has a brown belly and paw pads, white and black plastic eyes, white plush muzzle, black threaded nostrils and mouth, pink-lined ears, and a black fuzzy mane and tail tip. A blue plastic "safety pin" is mounted where the tail connects to the body. The gold and red plush Baby Pooh has black plastic eyes, a brown pom-pom nose, and black threaded eyebrows and mouth. A faux flap is sewn onto Pooh's backside to mimic baby clothing. Baby Pooh items were sold at the Disney parks. Each are 10in (25cm) in height. Mint condition: **$20-35** each. Jolly Toys Inc., circa mid-1970s. 5in (13cm) cloth blocks decorated with Pooh pictures on one side, sold through Sears. Shown are Pooh with dynamite and Pooh with a jack-in-box (rattle inside). Not shown is Pooh playing baseball. Very good condition: **$40-50** set of three.

48. Simon Marketing Inc., circa 1987-1989. A set of three plush Pooh characters dressed in Christmas apparel were sold at a very limited number of McDonalds restaurants. *Left:* Two-toned gray 7in (18cm) Eeyore has black and white plastic eyes, black threaded nostrils, and a pink and red cloth mouth. He is wearing a green scarf with red fringe and a red felt hat with green felt trim. *Center:* Pale yellow plush 8in (20cm) Pooh wearing a

red and white stocking hat and red, yellow, blue plaid vest. Pooh has black threaded eyebrows, a black plastic nose and eyes, and a red cloth mouth. *Right:* The orange and black striped Tigger has a cream colored belly, muzzle, eye and ear linings, black felt eyes, a pink cloth nose, and a rust-colored cloth mouth and bottom paw pads. Tigger is wearing a removable red and black plaid flannel shirt with Velcro closure. 8in (20cm). Near mint condition: **$35-45** each.

49. Gund, Inc., circa 1992-1995. This red and gold terry cloth covered stuffed Baby Pooh has chimes inside. Pooh has black threaded eyebrows and mouth, black plastic eyes, and a black cloth nose. A small red collar is sewn into the neck seam. Baby Pooh items were sold at the Disney parks. 7in (18cm). Mint condition: **$15-20**.

50. Anne Wilkinson Designs Ltd. (England), circa early 1990s. The gray stuffed Eeyore is manufactured from quilted material and has a light blue underside and ear lining, printed facial features, and a black yarn mane and tail tip. His tail is not removable. 16in (41cm) long, 11in (28cm) tall. Mint condition: **$75-125**.

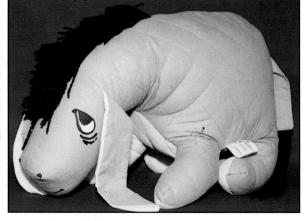

51. Gabrielle Designs Limited (England), circa 1992-1993. This set of larger dolls was Gabrielle's first set of Pooh characters. Attached to all of the animals are paper cards containing an E.H. Shepard illustration and a verse from Pooh literature pertaining to that character. *Left to right:* The 12in (31cm) long by 8in (20cm) tall gray fuzzy Eeyore has a black yarn mane and tail tip and two-tone brown teardrop plastic eyes on a black felt background. His tail is removable via a button. Mint condition: **$75-90**. The gold, black, and white striped corduroy sitting Tigger has stripes and facial features (other than the eyes) that are painted on the cloth. Tigger's eyes are black plastic on a white vinyl background. 13in (33cm). Mint condition: **$85-100**. The honey-colored plush Pooh is wearing a red sweater vest. He has jointed legs, black plastic eyes and nose, brown threaded eyebrows, and brown suede-like ear linings and paw pads. 14in (36cm). Mint condition: **$100-125**. The pink felt Piglet wears a green and black knit shirt, and holds purple felt violets. Piglet is bean-bag stuffed, and has black plastic eyes and a dark green scarf. 7in (18cm). Mint condition: **$50-70**. The brown and white suede-like Kanga (13in [33cm]) has a 6in (15cm) removable Roo in her pocket. Both have black plastic eyes. Kanga has a black plastic nose. Mint condition: **$75-90**.

52. Anne Wilkinson Designs Ltd (England), circa 1993. This Pooh pajama case depicts a yellow Pooh tucked into a cloth red and white striped bed. Pooh has black printed eyes, a black cloth nose, a black threaded mouth, and is wearing a red and white striped stocking hat. 11in (28cm) by 15in (38cm). Mint condition: **$45-60**.

53. Carousel by Guy, Inc., circa 1990-1991. This Pooh pajama bag was sold through The Disney Store. The orange-yellow plush is sewn into the red shirt. White "Pooh" lettering is printed on the shirt. Pooh has black plastic eyes, a black pom-pom nose, and a red cloth mouth. There is a zipper along the back for pajamas, in addition to black straps for backpack use. 18in (46cm) from head to rump. Mint condition: **$35-45**.

54. Carousel by Guy, Inc., circa 1990-1991. This Tigger pajama bag was sold through The Disney Store. Tigger consists of an orange and black striped plush with pale yellow belly, muzzle, and eye background plush. He has thick black eyebrows, black plastic eyes, a brown stuffed nose, and a brown mouth. There is a zipper along the back for pajamas, in addition to black straps for backpack use. 18in (46cm) from head to rump. Mint condition: **$35-50**.

55. Carousel by Guy, Inc., circa 1990-1991. This Eeyore pajama bag was sold through The Disney Store. Eeyore consists of a medium gray plush with a light gray underside and muzzle. He has black plastic eyes, brown cloth nostrils, and a black fuzzy mane and tail tip. There is a zipper along the back for pajamas, in addition to black straps for backpack use. 18in (46cm) from head to rump. Mint condition: **$35-45**.

56. Wendy Lawton, circa 1995. This limited edition (100 pieces) set of Christopher Robin and Pooh was sold at the 1995 Walt Disney World Teddy Bear Convention. Christopher Robin (13in [33cm]) is porcelain and wears a blue and white striped smock and shorts. The shorts are sewn to a white shirt. He is also wearing a beige hat, socks, and shoes. The 6in (15cm) felt-covered Pooh is jointed and wears a red shirt. His eyes are black glass, and he has black threaded eyebrows, nose and mouth. Mint condition in original box **$850-1000**.

57. Steiff, circa 1994. The fully-jointed honey-colored mohair Pooh was sold at the 1994 Walt Disney World Teddy Bear Convention in a limited edition of 2500 pieces. Pooh is wearing a maroon knit vest and has black glass eyes and a black threaded nose and mouth. The Steiff button and tag is in his left ear. 12in (30cm). Mint condition: **$600-800**.

58. Gund Mfg, Inc., circa 1995. The dark brown deep-piled plush Festival Pooh was sold at the 1995 Walt Disney World Teddy Bear Convention in a limited edition of 300 pieces. He has black button eyes and a black threaded nose. Pooh is wearing a maroon sweater vest fastened with a single wooden button. He is partially stuffed with bean-bag material to weight his bottom. This pattern appears to be the same that Gund used for their 1991 Teddy Bear Convention Pooh. Mint condition (was not packaged in a box): **$125-150**.

59. Canasa Trading Corp., circa 1995. This yellow plush Pooh was offered in small numbers for a very short time through The Disney Store. Covered with yellow plush, he is wearing a straw hat trimmed with green ribbon, a dusty rose shirt and slate blue overalls with yellow "Pooh" embroidered on the front pocket. Pooh has black threaded eyebrows, black button eyes, a black velvet-covered hard nose, and a red cloth mouth. 14in (35cm). Mint condition: **$50-85**.

60. Gabrielle Designs Limited (England), circa 1993-1994. Attached to this set of smaller animals, are paper cards containing an E.H. Shepard illustration and a verse from Pooh literature pertaining to that character. The cards are the same as those used with Gabrielle's larger set of dolls. From left to right: The brown and white stuffed 10in (25cm) Kanga has black plastic eyes and nose and carries brown and white 5in (13cm) Roo with black plastic eyes in her pocket. Mint condition: **$50-60**. The gold acrylic plush Pooh is wearing a red sweater vest and has jointed legs, black plastic eyes and nose, black threaded eyebrows, brown paw pads and ear linings. Mint condition: **$50-70**. Pink felt 5in (13cm) Piglet wears a green and black sweater and a dark green scarf, and holds purple felt violets. Piglet has black beaded eyes. Mint condition: **$40-50**. Dark gray suede-like Eeyore has a black yarn mane and tail tip and two-tone brown eyes on black felt background. His eyes are teardrop shaped and his tail is removable via a button. 9in (23cm) long, 6in (15cm) tall. Mint condition: **$50-60**. The gold corduroy Tigger is painted with black and white stripes, nose and mouth. He has black plastic eyes on white vinyl circles. 11in (28cm) sitting. Mint condition: **$50-60**.

61. Anne Wilkinson Designs Ltd. (England), circa early 1990s. The yellow cotton Pooh pajama bag has Velcro closures in the back. Pooh is wearing a red cotton shirt, and has black printed eyes, a black cloth nose, and a black threaded mouth. 24in (61cm). Mint condition: **$75-85**.

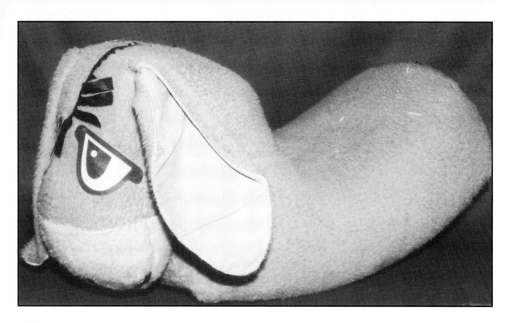

62. Sears, circa 1976-1978. The gray stuffed Eeyore rocker is mounted on a curved wooden base. Eeyore has a blue muzzle and ear linings, a black felt mane, black felt eyebrows, black felt nostrils and mouth, and black and white paper eyes. 11in (28cm) high, 22in (56cm) long. Very good condition: **$100-125**.

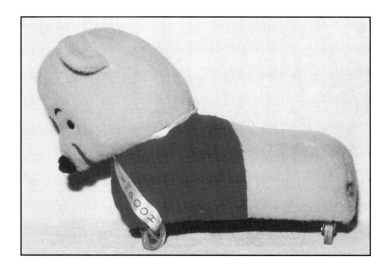

63. Commonwealth Toy & Novelty Co. Inc., circa mid-1970s. Pictured is a gold and red plush Pooh riding toy. Pooh's head and rear portions of his body are covered with gold plush; the front half of the body is covered with red plush material. Pooh has black plastic eyes, black felt eyebrows, a black pom-pom nose, and a red felt mouth. A yellow ribbon printed with "Winnie the Pooh" lettering is sewn into the neck in a later version but in an early '70s version, Pooh wore a red bib with his name written in white. Four clear plastic wheels are mounted on the bottom. This item was sold through Sears. 14in (36cm) high, 18in (46cm) long. Very good condition: **$100-150**.

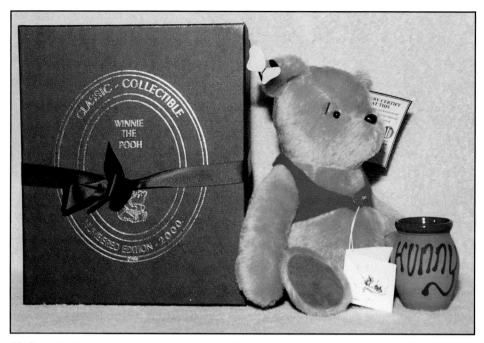

64. Gabrielle Designs Limited (England), circa 1993. The limited edition (2,000 pieces) mohair 11in (28cm) Pooh is wearing a red sweater vest, and has black plastic eyes and nose, brown threaded eyebrows, and brown suede bottom paw pads. A "pip-cleaner" type bee sits on his right ear. Pooh comes with a hand-thrown honey pot and is packaged in a forest green box. Mint condition in original box: **$125-150**.

65. Canasa Trading Corp, circa 1993. This large plush pink Piglet was sold through The Disney Store in London, England. Piglet's sewn-in shirt is purple with black stripes. Piglet has black plastic eyes, black threaded eyebrows and mouth, and a pink plush nose. While the design of Piglet is the same as sold in the United States, this size (16in [41cm]) has not yet been available here. Mint condition: **$55-70**.

66. Canasa Trading Corp., circa 1991-1992. The yellow plush Pooh backpack has a red shirt and red pack decorated with white "Pooh" lettering. The pack is sewn into Pooh's back. Pooh has black plastic eyes, a black velveteen nose, and a black mouth. It was sold at the Disney parks. 14in (36cm). Mint condition **$35-45**.

67. Carousel by Michaud, circa 1992. The limited edition (100 pieces) Pooh was sold at the 1992 Walt Disney World Teddy Bear Convention. He is constructed of brown mohair, wears a red shirt, and has jointed legs, black plastic eyes and nose, and a black threaded mouth. 10in (25cm) sitting. Mint condition in original box: **$325-350**.

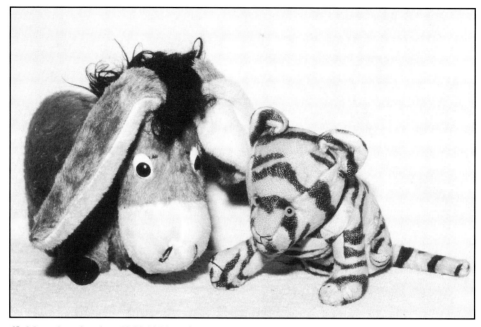

68. Merrythought, circa 1966-1976. *Left:* The plush gray Eeyore has a white muzzle, pink ear linings, black cloth hooves, black threaded mouth, nostrils, and eyebrows, black fuzzy mane and tail tip, and white and black plastic eyes. The tail snaps on and off. The tag is sewn onto Eeyore's right rear foot. 12in (30cm) long. Excellent condition: **$400-450**. *Right:* The orange and dark brown striped Tigger has wire-reinforced front legs and neck, amber and black glass eyes, and a black threaded nose and mouth. 9in (23cm) long, 7in (18cm) tall. Good condition: **$250-275**; Excellent condition: **$400-450**.

69. Burbank (England), circa late 1970s-early 1980s. The shaggy tan plush Pooh has black cloth paw pads on feet, black threaded eyebrows and mouth, black plastic eyes, and a black cloth nose. 12in (31cm). Very good condition: **$50-75**.

70. *Left:* Burbank (England), circa late 1970s-early 1980s. Shaggy tan plush Pooh hand puppet whose body is lightly stuffed to allow a small hand through the open back. Pooh has brown paw pads, a red shirt, black plastic eyes, and black threaded nose and mouth. 11in (28cm). Excellent condition: **$75-100**. *Right:* Marks & Spencer (England), circa unknown. Gold plush Pooh with black paw pads has a black cloth nose, black threaded mouth, black velvet eyes, and a red shirt with white vinyl lettering. 10in (25cm). Excellent condition: **$75-100**.

71. Canasa Trading Corp, circa 1993. This large plush gray and white Eeyore was sold through the Disney Store in London, England. Eeyore has black and white plastic eyes, black embroidered eyebrows and nostrils, pink ear linings and bow on tail, and a black furry mane and tail tip. While the design of Eeyore is the same as sold in the United States, this size (20in [51cm]) has not yet been available here. Mint condition: **$90-120**.

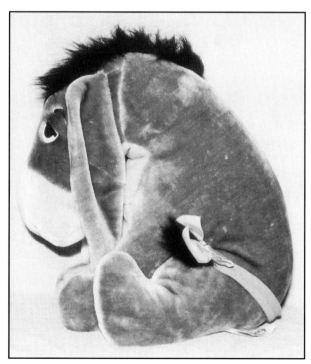

72. Gund, Inc., circa 1993. These yellow soft plush Poohs are wearing red removable shirts decorated with gold "Pooh" lettering. Gold musical notes decorate the musical Pooh who plays the Winnie the Pooh theme song when the music button near his chest is pressed. Each Pooh has black plastic eyes, a black plush nose, black threaded eyebrows, and a red cord mouth. These were sold through Sears. *Left:* 15in (38cm). Mint condition: **$20-30**. Center: Musical 10in (25cm). Mint condition: **$25-35**. *Left:* 22in (56cm). Mint condition: **$35-45**.

73. Carrousel by Michaud, circa 1994. The limited edition (100 pieces) "And A Partridge in a Pooh Tree" was sold at the 1994 Walt Disney World Teddy Bear Convention. The fully-jointed 13in (33cm) standing Pooh is made out of honey-colored mohair, and is dressed in a red jacket and scarf and a red hat trimmed with white. Pooh has black threaded eyebrows and mouth, black plastic eyes and nose, and brown felt paw pads. Included is an 11in (28cm) artificial fir tree housing a small brown, white, and yellow bird. The base of the tree is wrapped in burlap. Mint condition in original box: **$325-350**.

74. *Left:* Mothercare (England), circa 1994. The tan stuffed Pooh is holding a rust-colored stuffed "hunny" pot. Pooh has black threaded facial features. 12in (31cm). Mint condition: **$65-75**. *Right:* Mothercare (England), circa 1994. The pink stuffed Piglet has a green and black sewn-in shirt and black threaded eyes. 7in (18cm) Mint condition: **$35-45**.

75. Sun and star, circa 1992-1994. The gold plush Pooh is wearing a red removable shirt, and has black plastic eyes, a brown plastic nose, black vinyl eyebrow, and black threaded mouth. He was sold at the Japan Pavilion in the World Showcase at Epcot, Lake Buena Vista, Florida. 8in (20cm) sitting. Mint condition: **$25-35**.

76. California Stuffed Toys, Distributed by Pedigree Dolls and Toys Ltd (England), circa 1970s. *Left:* 9in (23cm) seated tan plush Pooh has black button eyes, a black pom-pom nose, and red threaded mouth. Excellent condition: **$50-65**. *Right:* Seated 7in (18cm) two-toned gray Eeyore has a black fuzzy mane and tail tip, black felt nostrils and eyebrows (missing in this example), three-part gray, white, and black felt eyes, and pink cloth ear linings. Very good condition: **$50-65**.

77. Sears, circa late 1970s-early 1980s. The yellow plush Pooh head pajama bag has a red cloth backside. Pooh has black felt facial features and zipper along neck. 14in (36cm) tall. Very good condition: **$25-35**.

78. Merrythought, circa 1966-1976. *Left:* Gold mohair Pooh is fully jointed and has a black threaded mouth and nose with amber and brown button eyes. His paw pads are covered with light brown cloth. His original red shirt with white "Pooh" letters is missing. 14in (36cm). Excellent condition: **$275-325** without shirt, **$450-550** with shirt. *Right:* Pink felt-covered Piglet is wearing blue pants and suspenders, a red shirt, and a plaid scarf. He is missing his original jacket. His eyes are black and white plastic, and his eyebrows and nose are inked onto the cloth. He has a curly tail and molded feet. The tag is located on the bottom of the left foot. 11in (28cm). Very good condition: **$300-350** without original jacket, **$400-450** with jacket.

79. Canterbury Bears (England), circa 1995. This limited edition (250 pieces) jointed, yellow mohair Pooh is holding a long stick for which to play Poohsticks. He has black glass eyes and black threaded eyebrows, nose, and mouth. He is wearing a maroon felt shirt fastened with a single white button. This edition was sold at the 1995 Walt Disney World Teddy Bear Convention. Mint condition (was not originally packaged in box): **$325-400**.

80. Canasa Trading Corp., circa 1995-1995. The gold plush Santa Pooh is wearing a red cotton shirt with gold "Pooh" letters embroidered on the chest. He is also wearing a red and white Santa hat and a white fuzzy beard. Pooh is holding a green cloth bag that is sewn to his shirt and right arm. His facial features include black threaded eyebrows, black plastic eyes, a hard black velvet covered nose, and a red cloth mouth. 11in (28cm) from rump to head. Mint condition: **$35-40**.

81. Carrousel by Michaud, circa 1993. Limited edition (100 pieces) Pooh sold at the 1993 Disney World Teddy Bear Convention. The jointed 13in (33cm) standing Nite Nite Pooh is made out of honey-colored mohair, and is dressed in a light blue night shirt and nightcap. Pooh has black threaded eyebrows and mouth, black plastic eyes and nose, and brown felt paw pads. Mint condition in original box: **$325-350**.

CHAPTER 2

CLOCKS, WATCHES, AND JEWELRY

CLOCKS

82. Clockwise Beverly Hills, circa 1990. The black glass wall clock is illustrated with Owl, Christopher Robin, Kanga and Roo, Tigger, Eeyore, Pooh, Piglet, and Rabbit marching through the 100 Acre Woods. 9 in (23cm) by 11in (28cm). It was sold through The Disney Store for a very limited time. Mint condition **$125-150**.

83. Sears, circa 1976-1977. This ceramic honey pot clock has a figural Owl and Pooh on each side. The honey pot sits on green grass and pink flowered ceramic base. 7in (18cm) long, 6in (15cm) tall. Near mint condition: **$200-275**.

84. Bradley, circa 1976. A 3in (8cm) square alarm clock manufactured with a plastic yellow casing and a plastic orange alarm button on the top. Pooh is pictured on the clock face; his arms point to the time. This is a less common version than the round Bradley Pooh clock described below. Excellent condition: **$85-125**.

85. Charpente, circa 1993. The top of this wooden clock is decorated with a cut-out of Pooh, whose head is stuck in a honey pot. The clock has a natural finish and is accented with two yellow decorative cords that hold blue beads at the bottom to mimic weights: 6-1/2in (17cm) x 5-1/2 (14cm). Mint condition: **$50-60**.

86. Shapes (England), circa 1994-1995. This fiberboard clock features classic-style Pooh with a blue honey pot on the clock face along with the inscription "Rumbly in your tumbly". About an inch in front of the clock face is a decorative wooden plate picturing Pooh's back with many honey pots and a balloon on a tree limb. 8in (20cm) x 6in (15cm). Mint condition: **$65-80**.

87. Reflex Marketing Ltd (England), circa 1995. A wooden frame encases a clock face using a copy of an original E.H. Shepard drawing. This particular one pictures Pooh and Piglet playing Poohsticks. Other drawings have been used in this series as well. 5in (13cm) square. Mint condition: **$55-70**.

88. MM's Designs Inc., circa 1990. The hand painted wooden clock is illustrated with a detailed picture of Pooh holding a blue balloon in front of his tree house. Bees and a honey pot are nearby. The coloring is in pastels. 12in (31cm) tall, 9in (23cm) wide. Mint condition. **$100-125**.

89. *Left:* Charpente, circa 1993. A bisque 7-3/4in (20cm) figural Pooh stands next to a 3in (8cm) diameter clock in the form of a pocket watch. The clock is battery operated. Pooh is a muted-yellow with a maroon shirt and is standing on green grass. Mint condition: **$85-100**. *Right:* Charpente, circa 1993. A bisque battery operated clock is inset into the beige background behind Christopher Robin and Pooh in bed. Honey pots sit atop a shelf above the clock face. Blue and mauve blankets cover Christopher Robin. Pooh is yellow. 6-1/2in (17cm) x 5-1/4in (13cm). Mint condition: **$65-85**.

90. Willitts, circa 1991. The ceramic bisque clock is characterized with an arching frame and characters in relief. The frame consists of a tree wrapping around a scene that contains Pooh and Piglet. The background of the clock is blue; Pooh is yellow; and Piglet is pink and lavender. Greenery surrounds the characters. 6-1/2in (17cm) x 7-1/4in (18cm). Mint condition: **$60-75**.

91. Phinney-Walker, circa 1969-1971. The face of this red and white plastic wall clock is illustrated with Pooh sitting next to a honey pot and holding a spoon. Three bees fly near Pooh's head. This clock was made in Germany and sold through Sears with accompanying record and storybook of "Winnie the Pooh and the Blustery Day". Phinney-Walker is a subsidiary of Hamilton Watch Company, SEMCA Time Corporation. 8in (20cm) diameter. Excellent condition: **$75-100**.

92. Armstrong & Claydon (England), circa 1991. A colorful metal clock illustrated with a scene of Christopher Robin, Pooh, and Piglet playing Poohsticks from the bridge. This version was also sold in Belgium. 8in (20cm) diameter. Mint condition: **$70-85**.

93. Tokyo Disneyland, circa 1992. The glossy ceramic clock features a figural Pooh climbing a rockery to reach a honey pot on the other side. Much of the clock is tan with brown and green accents. Pooh is gold with a red shirt. Two bees are pictured on the face of the clock. 6in (15cm) high. Mint condition: **$125-200**.

94. Gumbridge (England), circa 1995. The tin clock features classic style Christopher Robin and Pooh going down the stairs. 8in (20cm) in diameter. Mint condition: **$55-75**.

95. Sunbeam, circa 1994-1995. The same face design is found on either a red-trimmed plastic wall clock (8-1/2in [22cm] diameter) or a red metal double bell alarm clock (4in [10cm] diameter). The design features Pooh in the center of the clock face, with the faces of Rabbit, Piglet, Eeyore, and Tigger along the outer edges. On the wall clock, a bee revolves on the end of the second hand. These were sold through The Disney Store. Mint condition, wall clock: **$20-30**. Mint condition, alarm clock: **$20-30**.

96. *Left:* Walt Disney Productions, circa 1994. A yellow plastic Pooh wearing a red shirt holds a large blue honey pot that houses a musical clock. Bees rotate on a plastic disk within the clock face. A bee atop the honey pot is a switch for the alarm which plays the Winnie the Pooh theme song. While most musical Pooh toys play only the song's chorus, this clock plays the verse as well. 5in (13cm). Mint condition: **$50-60**. *Right:* Tokyo Disneyland, circa 1992. A plastic green base supports a plastic tan stump housing a clock next to a yellow figural Pooh wearing a red shirt. Pooh holds a brown and gold honey pot. When the alarm is activated, Pooh moves the honey pot to and from his mouth while a Japanese phrase is repeated. 7-1/2in (19cm). Mint condition: **$150-175**.

97. Sears, circa 1976. A blue and white plastic wall clock illustrated with Pooh sleeping under a tree next to a honey pot. 11in (28cm) diameter. Excellent condition: **$75-100**.

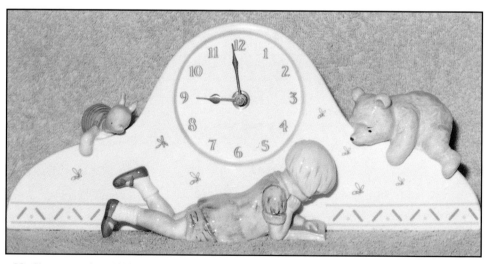

98. Charpente, circa 1993-1994. The glossy ceramic clock has a white casing and features figural Christopher Robin reading a book at the base, with Pooh and Piglet hanging at each end of the clock. 13in (33cm) x 6in (15cm). Mint condition: **$75-100**.

99. Clockwise Beverly Hills, circa 1990. The black glass wall clock is illustrated with Owl, Christopher Robin, Kanga and Roo, Tigger, Eeyore, Pooh, Piglet, Rabbit, and Gopher near Piglet's house. 9in (23cm) x 11in (28cm). It was sold through The Disney Store for a very limited time. Mint condition: **$125-150**.

100. Bradley, circa 1974-1976. A round alarm clock with a yellow metal casing and orange alarm bells featuring Pooh pointing to the time. 4in (10cm) tall. Excellent condition: **$75-100**.

WATCHES

101. Tokyo Disneyland, circa 1990. The watch face is illustrated with a yellow Pooh near three brown honey pots. He is wearing a red shirt and holding red flowers. The watch has a gold metal casing and a brown leather band. A watch very similar to this, was sold in the United States a couple of years later (see below). Mint condition **$75-100**.

102. Apollo (England), circa 1987. A black and yellow silhouetted watch face is illustrated with Pooh and Piglet walking under the moon and stars. Near mint condition: **$100-150**.

103. Alba (Tokyo Disneyland), circa 1992. This gold watch face is etched with outlines of Pooh and Piglet standing near a honey pot, while Pooh holds a second pot. Mint condition: **$100-150**.

104. Tokyo Disneyland, circa 1989-1990. On this colorful watch face, Pooh is standing with a honey pot on his head, and reaching out to Piglet, who is holding another honey pot. The watch has a gold metal casing and leather band. Mint condition: **$150-200**.

105. The Walt Disney Company, circa 1993-1994. This watch face features Pooh thinking of each of his friends. The friends are pictured on a revolving disk with only one character showing at any one time through a window to the upper left of Pooh. The other characters include: Rabbit, Eeyore, Tigger, Owl, Kanga and Roo, and Piglet. A different character appears in Pooh's thoughts about every two hours. A honey pot and two bees are pictured near Pooh. The watch has a brown leather band and a metal casing. Mint condition: **$75-100**.

106. The Walt Disney Company, circa 1994. This watch face has a black background with gold numbers, and features Pooh, wearing a blue nightshirt and cap, sleeping next to Piglet. Piglet is wearing a pink nightshirt and cap. Revolving through a window on the left are gold stars, moon and sun. The watch has a metal casing and black leather band. Mint condition: **$65-75**.

107. Bradley, circa 1974. This extremely rare early digital Pooh watch was sold through Sears and has a watch face illustrated with Pooh sitting next to a honey pot and raising one arm. The time is shown in windows to the left of Pooh. Numbers rotate into the window to indicate the time. Excellent condition: **$200-300**.

108

109

110

111

112

113

108. Bradley, circa 1974-1975. The blue Time Teacher watch features a yellow Pooh wearing a red shirt and holding a brown honey pot. An extra set of 60 numbers are pictured in the outer margin of the blue watch face to more readily teach a child the number of minutes the watch hands are indicating. This watch was sold through Sears, and came with a sew-on patch featuring sitting Pooh with honey pot against a navy background and red "WINNIE THE POOH" stitched across the top. Excellent condition: **$125-150**.

109. Sears, circa 1965 (available through 1971). The watch face pictures a yellow Pooh, who is wearing a red shirt and standing, holding a brown honey pot. Two bees circle nearby. The lettering on the watch face is blue; the background is white. This watch was made by Timex for Sears. The original box included a ceramic Enesco Pooh figurine holding a blue styrofoam balloon. The Pooh figurine was standing on a green base. The box had a clear plastic display top. Very good condition without original figurine and box: **$125-150**. Very good condition with original figurine and box: **$250-300**.

110. Sears, circa 1970s. The orange and black striped Tigger is bouncing across this watch face, knocking over three honey pots on his way. The watch numbers are green. This watch is extremely rare and desirable. Near mint condition: **$350-500**.

111. Lorus, circa 1992. This watch has the same face design as the Tokyo Disneyland watch described above, but this watch has a red plastic casing and a red vinyl band. Mint condition: **$45-55**.

112. The Walt Disney Company, circa 1990. The watch face features a gold Pooh, wearing a red shirt, sleeping under a tree next to a honey pot. Bees are pictured near the honey pot, and "Zs" are written next to Pooh. The background scene pictures colorful green grass and a blue sky. The original box consisted of a white plastic base and a clear plastic top. Excellent condition: $65-80.

113. Tokyo Disneyland, circa 1990. The face of this watch features a yellow Pooh wearing a red shirt, sitting on green grass and taking honey out of a pot. Four other pots and three bees are nearby. The watch has a metal casing and brown leather band. Mint condition: **$100-125**.

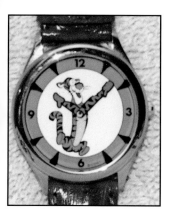  

Left: **114.** The Walt Disney Company, circa 1992-1993. The watch face features an orange and black striped Tigger, with a white belly and face, standing and pointing to the time with his hands. The outer number margin is orange, and some numbers are substituted by black stripes. The watch has a brown leather band. Mint condition: **$60-75**. *Center:* Disney Time Works, circa 1994. This watch is part of a series of "Lunchbox" watches sold at the Disney parks. It is a limited edition (5000 pieces) that was packaged in a small (5in [13cm] x 5-1/2in [14cm]) metal box (see page 59) decorated with colorful pictures of Pooh and his friends. Also included was a cloisonné Pooh pin. The watch face features Tigger, Eeyore, Pooh, and Piglet under a prism-cut crystal. The band is brown leather. Mint condition in the original box with pin: **$150-175**. *Right:* The Walt Disney Company, circa 1993. The watch face features Pooh sitting and eating honey from a nearby pot. Three bees revolve on a clear plastic disk. The watch has a metal casing and brown leather band. Mint condition: **$55-65**.

Below: Left: **115.** The Walt Disney Company, circa 1993. This limited edition (500 pieces) watch was available only to Disney Cast Members. The colorful watch face shows Pooh, Tigger, and Eeyore decked in Christmas garb with holly decorating the background. Piglet flies around the edge of the face on a clear plastic revolving disk. Written on the face is "Christmas 1993" "A Joyful Christmas Cast".

The watch has a leather band and metal casing. Mint condition: **$125-150**. *Center:* Time Works, circa 1994. Tigger's orange and black striped head and yellow muzzle and eye area decorates the watch face. The background is forest green. The watch has a metal casing and brown leather band. "Tigger" is embossed on the band. Mint condition: **$55**. *Right:* Lorus, circa 1992-1993. The watch face pictures Pooh eating honey while several bees revolve around him on a clear plastic disk. The brown leather band is embossed with bees. Mint condition: **$35-50**.

116. Ballanda Corp., circa 1994. This limited edition (400 pieces) watch was available to Disneyland Cast Members. The face features: Tigger wearing mouse ears and clutching a honey pot by a Disneyland sign: Pooh eating honey; and Piglet sitting on Pooh's head. Two bees are nearby, with another bee perched on the second hand. Written on the face is "Summer '94". The watch has a brown leather band, and was packaged in a wooden box inscribed with "A Hunny of a Time at Disneyland". Mint condition in original box: **$85-120**.

117. Sears, circa 1965. This wristwatch face is illustrated with Pooh carried by a blue balloon. Pooh is gold with a red shirt. Although the watch has a printed date of 1965, it was available through 1972. The original box included a ceramic Enesco Pooh figurine holding a blue styrofoam balloon. The Pooh figurine was standing on a green base. The outer box pictured the Pooh characters. Very good condition without original figurine and box: **$125-150**. Very good condition with original figurine and box: **$250-300**.

118. Apollo (England), circa 1987. A profile of the upper half of Pooh is pictured on this watch face. Pooh is eating honey with three bees nearby. This watch was first produced in England and commanded a high price on the collector's market in the United States. However, in the early 1990s, it was available at the Disney parks for half the previous cost. Mint condition: **$55-65**.

119. The Walt Disney Company, circa 1993. Decorating this watch face, is Pooh sitting and eating from a honey pot with two bees nearby. The watch has a tan plastic casing and tan vinyl band. Mint condition: **$35-40**.

120. Bradley, circa 1972-1975. Pooh is pictured on the watch face, while his arms point to the time. "Winnie the Pooh" is written at the top of the watch face. A similar watch was sold through Sears, and came with a sew-on patch featuring a sitting Pooh with honey pot against a navy background and red "WINNIE THE POOH" stitched across the top. Another similar watch was produced by Bradley in 1978 that shows Pooh in the same pose as above, only his arms are pictured at his sides and do not move. Very good condition: **$75-100**.

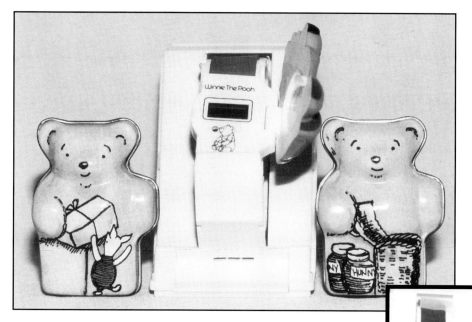

121. *Center:* Sears, circa 1988-1989. A white digital Pooh watch with a colorful plastic figural Pooh cover sold by Sears in the late 1980s, and reissued by The Disney Store (1992-1994). When the Pooh cover is flipped open to reveal the time, the Winnie the Pooh theme song plays. Pooh is also pictured in black and white near the digital read-out. Mint condition: **$10**. ***Left and Right:*** HunkyDory Designs (England), circa early 1990s. These tin figural tan Pooh containers have two different designs. One features Piglet and Pooh with a gift. The other depicts Pooh and honey pots. 2-1/2in (4cm). Near mint condition: **$15-20** each.

122. Fantasma, circa 1994. The watch face features Piglet sitting on Eeyore's back, and Eeyore's tail swings as the second hand. Rain clouds represent numerals along the sides, except for numeral 12 which is represented by the sun. "Find yourself a sunny day" is printed on the face. The watch has a gold metal casing and black leather band, and was packaged in a plastic blue and yellow honey pot. Mint condition in box: **$85-125**.

Top Left: **123.** Disney Time Works (Sutton Time), circa 1994-1995. This rectangular shaped face shows Pooh and Tigger eating honey with the time displayed in a small white circle in the background. The band is black vinyl and the watch was packaged in a velveteen pouch within a cardboard box. Mint condition: **$75-85.**

Top Right: **124.** Alba, circa 1993. This watch was sold at Toyko Disneyland and features Pooh standing against a white background. The watch casing is blue plastic and the band is blue vinyl. Mint condition: **$65-85.**

Left: **125.** Fossil Inc. (Disney Time Works), circa 1994-1995. This watch features Tigger bouncing out of a watch face. The band is brown leather, and the watch was packaged in a tin litho box decorated with Disney characters. Mint condition: **$75-85.**

Right: **126.** Disney Time Works, circa 1994-1995. On this watch face, Tigger is bouncing over the date box. The case is plated with titanium and the band is black leather. The packaging included a gray velveteen pouch in a cardboard box. Mint condition: **$65-75.**

127. Disney Time Works, circa 1994. This watch was sold at the Walt Disney World Resort and its face is decorated with Pooh, Tigger, and Piglet against a blue background. The band is vinyl and features colorful pictures of the same three characters against a green background. Mint condition: **$25-40**.

128. Disney Time Works, circa 1994. This watch is part of a series of "Lunchbox" watches sold at the Disney parks. It is a limited edition (5,000 pieces) that was packaged in a small (5in [13cm] x 5-1/2in [14cm]) metal box decorated with colorful pictures of Pooh and his friends. Also included was a cloisonné Pooh pin. The watch face features Tigger, Eeyore, Pooh, and Piglet under a prism-cut crystal (see page 55, top center). The band is brown leather. Mint condition in the original box with pin: **$150-175**.

JEWELRY

129. Walt Disney Productions, circa 1960s. This necklace holds a painted wooden 2in (5cm) Pooh figurine on gold chain. Pooh is orange with a red shirt and black facial features. Near mint condition: **$55-75**.

130. Walt Disney Productions, circa 1960s. The gold-plated metal charm bracelet holds painted figurines of Eeyore, Piglet, Pooh and Kanga with Roo in pocket. Because the paint readily flakes, it is rare to find paint still on the charms. Excellent condition: $**65-75**.

131. Walt Disney Productions, circa 1960s. This is a larger version of the above charm bracelet that includes: Pooh, Eeyore, Piglet, Kanga and Roo, Owl, and Rabbit as charms. Very good condition: **$75-95**.

132. Walt Disney Productions, circa 1980s. The metal charm bracelet holds pewter coins featuring the Pooh characters in relief. The characters include: Eeyore, Tigger, Piglet, Pooh, Kanga and Roo, Owl, and Rabbit. Mint condition: **$100-125**.

CHAPTER 3

LAMPS AND NIGHTLIGHTS

133. Dolly Toy Co (sold through Sears), circa 1966-1971. This lamp has a green plastic base and ceramic bisque tree trunk to support the shade. A bisque Pooh is climbing the tree with bisque figurines of Eeyore, Kanga, Roo, and Piglet watching. The original parchment paper shade is beige, decorated with pictures of bees and flowers. Another version was manufactured around 1978, identical in style, but the tree trunk and characters were manufactured from plastic. The same shade was used in both versions. 16in (41cm). Excellent condition with original shade: **$70-85**. Excellent condition without shade: **$45-65**.

134. Sears, circa early 1980s. This lamp consists of vinyl figurines of Pooh and Eeyore standing near vinyl letters of "POOH" that form the light stand. Excellent condition, without original shade: **$45-60**.

135. Dolly Toy Co (sold through Sears), circa 1969. This lamp has a walnut colored plastic base, a plastic open Pooh book in the background, and ceramic figures of Eeyore and Pooh holding a red styrofoam balloon with a bee atop the balloon. The Eeyore figurine is bisque, while the Pooh figurine is glossy ceramic. The original parchment paper shade is identical to the lamp described above. A 3-way switch allows a choice of lamp light, nightlight behind book, or both. 16in (41cm). Very good condition with original shade: **$80-95**. Very good condition without shade: **$45-65**.

136. Sears, circa 1976-1977. This table lamp has a glossy ceramic base forming a log under a tree. The tree supports the shade. Tigger (5in [13cm]) and Pooh are sitting on the log. Pictures of the 100 Acre Woods are printed on the original tan shade. 16in (41cm) overall. Mint condition with original shade: **$150-175**; without shade: **$85-100**.

137. Sears, circa late 1970s. A large vinyl Pooh holds a honey pot and sits on the base of this lamp. Two types of parchment paper shades were manufactured for this lamp, and both are shown above. A 3-way switch allows a choice of lamp light, a nightlight inside vinyl Pooh, or both. 16in (41cm). Excellent condition with original shade: **$45-55**.

138. Sears, circa 1980s. The 100 Acre Woods scene is printed on this cloth covered hanging lamp shade. While the background is white, green trees, grass, and colorful characters complete the scene. The shade is trimmed with gold-colored vinyl, and matches bedding and curtains also sold through Sears. Excellent condition: **$45-50**.

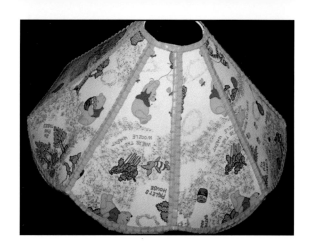

139. Sears, circa 1978-1980. A glass ceiling light cover depicting Pooh holding colorful balloons, Mint condition: **$50-85**.

140. Sears, circa 1978-1980. A glass light cover with Pooh and Piglet, Pooh and Tigger, Pooh and Rabbit, and Pooh and Eeyore. Mint condition: **$50-85**.

141. Sears, circa 1990-1992. A plush yellow Pooh wearing a red shirt sits on a white plastic base under a cloth-covered shade decorated with all of the Pooh characters. Mint condition: **$45-55**.

142. Charpente, circa 1992-1993. This lamp has a glossy ceramic base and figurines of Christopher Robin reading to Pooh. The shade is white with blue and gold trim at the bottom. Mint condition: **$85-100**.

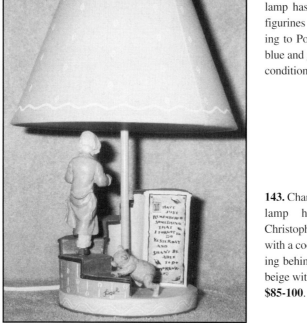

143. Charpente, circa 1992-1993. This lamp has bisque figurines of Christopher Robin walking upstairs with a cookie in hand and Pooh crawling behind him. The original shade is beige with white trim. Mint condition: **$85-100**.

144. Sears, circa 1974-mid 1980s. A musical lamp features a hard vinyl Pooh holding several plastic balloons. The colorful balloons surround the light bulb and serve as the lampshade. In earlier versions, the green honey pot in front of Pooh winds to play music. In later versions, the honey pot serves as a nightlight. Excellent condition: **$45-70**.

145. Mms Designs, Inc., circa 1989. The handcrafted wooden lamp features a figural wooden Pooh holding a honey pot. The original parchment shade is white with a blue balloon and bees. The paint is detailed and colored with pastels. Mint condition: **$100-125**.

146. Sears, circa 1980. This lamp has a plastic base supporting vinyl figurines of Eeyore pulling a wagon containing Pooh. The original parchment paper shade depicts Eeyore pulling a cart. Excellent condition with shade: **$50-65**; without shade: **$35-45**.

147. Charpente, circa 1994. These bisque figural nightlights feature two designs with Pooh and Piglet. *Left:* Pooh is pushing a cart containing two honey pots, and Piglet is standing near the front of the cart. The base is inscribed with "Now then Pooh. Time for a little something.". 6in (15cm) x 5-1/2in (14cm). *Right:* Pooh is reading to Piglet perched upon three books with a candle. 6in (15cm) x 6-1/2in (17cm). Mint condition: **$45-60** each.

148. Charpente, circa 1993. A bisque figural nightlight of Pooh holding a dripping honey to his mouth with Piglet nearby. 5in (13cm). Mint condition **$40-55**.

149. Charpente, circa 1994. These bisque figural nightlights of Pooh and Piglet are shown in two different styles. *Left:* Pooh and Piglet are wearing nightcaps and standing near a stump. The base is inscribed "Looking for Heffalumps". 6in (15cm) by 7in (18cm). *Right:* Pooh is tucked into bed with Piglet reading a book. A candle sits on the nearby night table. Mint condition: **$45-60** each.

CHAPTER 4

FIGURINES

150. Enesco, 1964. These glossy ceramic bookends feature Rabbit pushing Pooh through Rabbit's door, while Christopher Robin is pulling on Pooh arms. 4-1/2in (11cm) x 8in (20cm). Mint condition: **$225-300**.

151. Sears, circa 1976-1977. This glossy ceramic musical Pooh figurine revolves to the "Winnie the Pooh" theme song. Pooh is dancing among flowers on a round base. A honey pot is in the foreground. 6in (15cm). Mint condition: **$150-200**.

152. Palitoy (England), circa probably 1960s. The soft vinyl Pooh doll is 12in (31cm) tall and fully-jointed. The shirt in the photograph is probably not original. Pooh is tan-colored, has imprinted paw pads, and has sleep eyes rimmed with eyelashes. Very good condition: **$150-200**.

153. *Left:* Cavalier (England), circa 1960s. The Pooh bank is an uncommon silver-plated figure characterized by a shirt inscribed with "Pooh Bear". Pooh is holding a small dripping honey pot. 5in (13cm). Very good condition: **$45-60**. *Right:* Barton and Reed, circa late 1980s- early 1990s. A silver-plated bank of Pooh holding a honey pot widely sold in the United States. 5in (13cm). Mint condition: **$75-85**.

154. Sears, circa 1970s. This plastic yellow Pooh bank depicts Pooh holding a yellow honey pot. Pooh is sitting on a brown plastic stump, and is wearing a red shirt. 6in (15cm). Near mint condition: **$45-60**.

155. Buzza Cardozo, circa 1968-1972. These vinyl inflatable Pooh and Tigger Huff 'N Puffs originally sold as greeting "cards" with envelopes. *Left:* Pooh is tan with a red shirt and holds a brown honey pot containing a bell. "Have a honey of a birthday" is printed on the honey pot. 14in (36cm). *Right:* Tigger is bright orange with black stripes and squeaks when squeezed. "Feelin' better? Grrrreat!" is printed on his torso. Original Tigger package shown. 14in (36cm). Excellent condition: **$45-60** each.

156. Enesco, circa 1964. These glossy ceramic mugs feature Pooh and Kanga with Roo with relief lettering that states, "I'm Pooh" or "We're Kanga & Roo". In this version, Pooh is standing and does not hold a balloon. Excellent condition: **$50-75** each.

157. Sears, circa 1976-1977. Musical ceramic figurine of Eeyore pulling a circus cage containing Tigger with Pooh pushing the cage. Tigger revolves when wound. The figurine plays the "Winnie the Pooh" theme song. 10in (25cm) x 7in (18cm). Near mint condition: **$200-275**.

158. Schmid, circa early 1980s. The glossy ceramic figurine of Pooh and Christopher Robin revolves to the tune of "Talk to the Animals" Christopher Robin is writing "Pooh" in the dirt. 6in (15cm) x 4-1/2 (11cm). Near mint condition: **$150-200**.

159. The Walt Disney Company, circa 1993. This glossy ceramic teapot is in the form of a honey pot with Pooh as the pot's handle and Piglet as the lid's handle. It is dusty rose in color with yellow honey pouring out the top. Piglet is pink and Pooh is yellow with a red shirt. 7in (18cm). Mint condition: **$40-55**.

160. Hudson, circa 1988. This bisque figure depicts Owl's house in a gnarled tree. The piece was intended to accompany the Pooh pewter figurines made by Hudson. 6in (15cm) tall. Mint condition: **$125-150**.

161. Boots (England), circa 1989. The ceramic cream-colored Pooh honey jar depicts Pooh holding a honey pot. The jar separates at Pooh's waist for access. 7in (18cm). Mint condition: **$100-125**.

162. *Left:* Viceroy (Canada), circa 1980s. This is an uncommon vinyl squeeze toy of Pooh sitting on a stump holding a honey pot. A unique characteristic of this vinyl is the laugh wrinkles that surround the outer edge of Pooh's eyes. 7-1/2in (19cm). Excellent condition: **$40-50**. *Center:* Birds (England), circa 1970s. This uncommon vinyl figure bank depicts Pooh standing and eating honey. "Hunny Pudding" is written on honey pot. The bank ("money box") was a premium from Birds Dessert Mix, a banana or raspberry flavored mix with "real honey" to which one would add milk. 7-1/2in (19cm). Excellent condition: **$55-75**. *Right:* Walt Disney Productions (sold through The Disney Store and The Disney Catalog), circa 1993-1994. A vinyl 6in (15cm) bank of Pooh holding a spilled pot of honey. Mint condition: **$10-20**.

163. K. Onishi M.D. Co., Ltd., circa early 1990s. These two white glass salt and pepper shakers feature Pooh cooking. They were sold as a set at the Japan Pavilion in the World Showcase at Epcot in Lake Buena Vista, Florida. 3in (8cm). Mint condition: **$15-20** set.

164. *Left:* Charpente, circa 1993, around Valentine's Day. Pooh and Piglet are sitting in a chair with heart-shaped box of candy. The blue chair is decorated with pink hearts and serves as a glossy ceramic bank. 4in (10cm) x 5in (13cm). Mint condition: **$35-40**. *Right:* Charpente, circa 1993. A glossy ceramic bank with Christopher Robin in a bathtub and Pooh sitting on the edge with a pink towel on a nearby stool. 4in (10cm) x 6in (15cm). Mint condition: **$25-35**.

165. *Left:* The Walt Disney Company, circa 1993. This yellow Pooh cookie jar shows Pooh with one hand in a honey pot and the other hand in his mouth. Pooh's head removes for jar access, and Pooh is wearing a red shirt. 12in (31cm). Mint condition: **$50-100**. *Right:* The Walt Disney Company, circa 1994. This glossy ceramic cookie jar is in the shape of Pooh's house. Surrounding the house are: Tigger standing on the eave of Pooh's roof; Owl standing below Tigger; Kanga with Roo in her pocket; Piglet and Pooh sitting on a log; Eeyore sleeping; and Rabbit pushing a cart full of carrots. 11in (28cm) tall. Mint condition. **$250-350**.

166. Tokyo Disneyland, circa 1993. A glossy ceramic coaster picturing Piglet reading to Pooh in his house. 6in (15cm) diameter. Mint condition: **$50-80.**

167. Tokyo Disneyland, circa 1994. A detailed bisque musical figurine scene from the 100 Acre Woods sits on a wooden base. Pooh, Piglet, and Tigger are near trees and honey pots. The figurine plays "It's a Small World." . 7in (18cm) x 7-1/2in (19cm). Mint condition: **$350.**

168. The Walt Disney Company, circa 1993. These were sold separately as a glossy ceramic 5-1/2in (14cm) Eeyore creamer and 6in (15cm) Piglet sugar jar. Eeyore is gray and white, while Piglet is pink with a yellow scarf and red shirt. Mint condition: **$50** each.

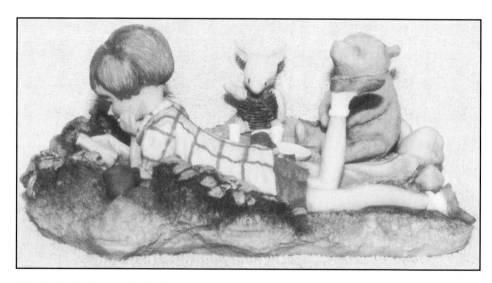

169. Arden Sculptures (England), circa 1994. A detailed bisque sculpture designed by Christopher Holt. "The Picnic" features Christopher Robin reading to Pooh and Piglet, who are surrounded by food. 8in (20cm) long. Available with or without wooden bases. Add $10 to the value if the wooden base is included. Mint condition without base: **$300**.

170. Arden Sculptures (England), circa 1994. Detailed bisque sculptures designed by Christopher Holt. *Left:* "Pooh got back to bed" shows Pooh sleeping in his bed with a green rug and pink slipper on the floor beneath him. 5in (13cm) long. Mint condition without wooden base: **$65-85**. *Right:* "Eeyore" depicts Eeyore tucking his head between his front legs to examine his tail. 4in (10cm) long Mint condition without base: **$45-65**. These figurines were originally available with or without wooden bases. Add $8 to the value of each piece if the wooden base is included.

171. Arden Sculptures (England), circa 1994. Detailed bisque sculptures designed by Christopher Holt. *Left:* "Piglet" features Piglet sitting among yellow flowers. 2in (5cm) tall. Mint condition without base: **$30-45**. *Right:* "Bath Mat" shows Pooh scratching his head while trying to read his bath mat. 4in (10cm) long. Mint condition without wooden base: **$40-55**. These figurines were originally available with or without wooden bases. Add $8 to the value of each piece if the wooden base is included.

77

172. *Left:* Tokyo Disneyland, circa 1994. This musical bisque figurine depicts Pooh, Tigger, Rabbit, and Piglet eating at a table. The figurine plays "Teddy Bear Picnic". The front of the base is inscribed with "Winnie the Pooh". 4-1/2 (11cm) x 5in (13cm). Mint condition **$165-180**. *Right:* Tokyo Disneyland, circa 1994 The bisque musical figurine features Tigger bouncing Pooh in front of the "Poohs Thotful Spot" sign. "Winnie The Pooh" is inscribed on the front of the base. The figurine plays "Teddy Bear Picnic". 4in (10cm) x 5in (13cm). Mint condition: **$125-150.**

173. *Left:* Tokyo Disneyland, circa 1994. The glossy ceramic figurine shows Pooh sitting on green grass, one hand is held upwards, the other holds a honey pot. A violet honey pot trimmed in pink and a yellow honey pot trimmed in navy are behind Pooh. The figurine plays the Winnie the Pooh theme. 5in (13cm) tall, 4in (10cm) diameter. Mint condition: **$75-100**. *Right:* Tokyo Disneyland, circa 1994. This musical bisque figurine features Eeyore sitting near Pooh, who is holding a honey pot. Three pots are on the nearby ground. The musical plays the Winnie the Pooh theme. The front of the base is inscribed with "Winnie the Pooh". 4in (10cm) wide and high. Mint condition: **$125-150.**

174. *Left:* Tokyo Disneyland, circa 1994. The glossy ceramic musical figurine features Pooh standing on a round base with one arm held upwards and the other hand clutching a brown honey pot. The figurine plays "Teddy Bear Picnic". 4-1/4in (11cm) tall, 3in (8cm) diameter. Mint condition: **$70-80**. *Right:* Tokyo Disneyland, circa 1994. The bisque musical figurine features Pooh standing on a round base with a spoon in one hand and a honey pot in the other hand. The figurine plays "Teddy Bear Picnic". 4-1/4in (11cm) tall, 3in (8cm) diameter. Mint condition: **$65-75**.

175. Maker unknown (England), circa 1960s. This plate features Pooh and Rabbit eating honey and condensed milk in color on a white background. 6in (15cm) diameter. Mint condition: **$70-100**.

176. Arden Sculptures (England), circa 1994. Detailed bisque sculptures designed by Christopher Holt. *Left:* "What's twice eleven" features Pooh standing on a stool to write on a blackboard. 5in (13cm) tall. *Right:* "Don't you think so little Piglet?" has Piglet and Eeyore standing near a stump and muddy place. 5-1/2in (15cm) long. These figurines were originally available with or without wooden bases. Add $8 to the value of each piece if the wooden base is included. Mint condition without base: **$75-90** each.

177. Arden Sculptures (England), circa 1994. Detailed bisque sculptures designed by Christopher Holt, called "Surrounded by water". Pooh is sitting in a tree with all of his honey pots while the flood rushes below. 9in (23cm) x 5in (13cm). Mint condition: **$160-180**.

178. R.R. Hill (England), circa 1994. Bisque figurines from left to right: Pooh is holding a blue balloon and standing next to Piglet. 4-1/4in (10cm). Mint condition: **$25-40**. Piglet is climbing up a brown fence where Pooh is sitting. 3in (8cm). Mint condition: **$25-40**. Pooh is sitting in front of a rock and a purple flower. 2-3/4in (7cm). Mint condition: **$15-30**.

179. R. R. Hill (England), circa 1994. *Left:* This bisque figurine shows Eeyore munching on the thistles that Pooh just sat upon. 3-1/2in (9cm) long. Mint condition: **$20-35**. *Right:* A bisque figurine of Pooh sitting on a log near a tree and campfire. 3in (8cm) long. Mint condition **$15-30** each.

180. Sears, circa 1988-1989. These jointed, flocked vinyl figurines are part of a set (see page 89) and consist of: brown and tan Owl, yellow Pooh wearing a red cotton shirt, pink Piglet wearing a purple and black striped cotton shirt, and gray Eeyore detailed with black "stitching". Sizes range from 3in (8cm) to 5in (13cm) in height. Mint condition: **$20-25** each. Very good condition: **$8-15** each.

181. *Left:* Tokyo Disneyland, circa 1994. Plastic windup Pooh can walk across a flat surface. Pooh is yellow and is holding a green honey pot. 3-1/2in (9cm). Mint condition: **$25-30**. *Right:* Tokyo Disneyland, circa 1993. The glossy ceramic bell features Pooh sitting on top of the handle. Pooh has a honey pot on his head and his hand on his belly. Cinderella's castle in Tokyo Disneyland is pictured on front of the bell. 4in (10cm). Mint condition: **$50-75**.

182. Ron Lee, circa 1992. This limited edition (2750 pieces) sculpture portrays Tigger bouncing Pooh. It is constructed of clay characters, 24K gold trim, and an onyx base. 5-1/2in (14cm). Mint condition: **$200-250**.

183. The Walt Disney Company, circa 1993. This pitcher is a glossy ceramic yellow Pooh figurine. Pooh has brown paw pads and is wearing a red shirt and holding a brown and yellow honey pot. A hole is on the honey pot for pouring fluid. Pooh's head removes to prepare the beverage. 8in (20cm). Mint condition: **$40-60**.

184. Richard G. Kruager, New York (Made in Germany), circa 1940. The yellow ceramic pitcher is a figural of Pooh with black painted features. Copyright on bottom is "Stephen Slesinger". 3in (8cm). Near mint condition: **$300-400**.

185. Schmid, circa early 1980s. The glossy ceramic figurine of Pooh and Piglet revolves to the tune of "Getting to Know You". Pooh and Piglet are near a spilled honey pot. 6in (15cm) x 4-1/2in (11cm). Near mint condition: **$150-200**.

186. The Walt Disney Company (made in Bavaria, sold in The Disney Store), circa 1993. A limited edition (1,000 pieces) Tigger figurine composed of 24% lead crystal. 4-1/2in (12cm). Mint condition: **$250-300**. In 1991, a similar edition (1,800 pieces) of crystal Pooh (not shown) was released. Mint condition: **$250-300**.

187. Tokyo Disneyland, circa 1994. The glossy ceramic musical features Pooh climbing out of a large honey pot. The figurine revolves to the "Winnie the Pooh" theme song. 4-1/2in (11cm) tall. Mint condition: **$75-100**.

188. The Walt Disney Company, circa 1992-1994. This glossy ceramic yellow Pooh sits on a white revolving musical base. "Winnie the Pooh" is inscribed on the base edge. Pooh is wearing a red shirt. This was sold through the Japan Pavilion in the World Showcase at Epcot in Lake Buena Vista, Florida. 3in (8cm) tall. Mint condition: **$30-45**.

189. The Walt Disney Company, circa 1993-1994. *Left:* Pooh and Eeyore are salt and pepper shakers. Cowboy Pooh is riding Gray Eeyore. 4in (10cm). Mint condition: **$35-45**. *Right:* Pooh and a balloon are salt and pepper shakers. Yellow Pooh is riding the blue balloon. 3in (8cm). Mint condition: **$35-45**.

190. Sears, circa 1980. These glossy ceramic figurines range from 1-1/4 (3cm) to 2-3/8in (6cm) in height. From left to right: blue and white standing Eeyore with black features; yellow and white Rabbit holding a blue honey pot; gold Pooh wearing a red shirt and holding a blue honey pot; orange and black striped dancing Tigger with a white belly, muzzle, eye and ear lining; seated pink Piglet, wearing a purple and black striped shirt and yellow scarf; brown and tan Owl standing with one wing in front. Mint condition: **$40-50** each.

191. Walt Disney Productions, circa 1992-1993. This glossy ceramic bank of Pooh eating honey was available in two sizes, 8in (20cm) and 5-1/2in (14cm). Mint condition 8in (20cm): **$25-35**. Mint condition 5-1/2in (14cm): **$15-25**.

192. Tokyo Disneyland, circa 1992-1993. Ceramic figurines from left to right: 2in (5cm) Pooh is crawling on a log; 2-1/2in (6cm) Pooh is eating honey; and 2in (5cm) Pooh, wearing a lavender nightshirt and cap, is holding a red book. Mint condition: **$45-60** each.

193. R. R. Hill (England), circa 1994. Bisque figurines left to right: Piglet visits Pooh who is stuck in Rabbit's hole. 2in (5cm) tall; Eeyore looks back at his tail. 2in (5cm) long; Pooh snoozes in a gray chair accented with pink flowers. 2in (5cm) tall. Mint condition: **$15-30** each.

194. United Design, circa 1991-1992. A set of six resin cast miniature figures that were sold at The Disney Store. Sizes range between 1—2in (3—5cm), and include: Eeyore sitting and looking back towards his tail; Piglet sitting on grass holding a yellow flower: Kanga and Roo hugging: Pooh and Piglet sitting on a bench; Tigger crouching in grass and reddish flowers; and Pooh sitting on grass near a basket. Mint condition: **$25-35** each.

195. Tokyo Disneyland, circa mid-1990s. These two white glass salt and pepper shakers each feature two different scenes. One shaker pictures Pooh and Piglet sitting on clouds near the castle on one side, with the other scene picturing two mouse ear balloons near a cloud. The second shaker pictures a castle on one side, and Pooh and Piglet floating among clouds and mouse ear balloons on the opposite side. "Tokyo Disneyland" is inscribed on both shakers. 3in (8cm). Mint in original box: **$65**.

196. R. R. Hill (England), circa 1994. Bisque figurines from left to right: Pooh and classic style Tigger are eating honey at a white table. 2in (5cm). Mint condition: **$25-40**. Pooh is sleeping on grass next to a basket and honey pots. 2-1/4in (5cm) long. Mint condition: **$15-30**. Kanga is bouncing along with Piglet in her pocket. 2-1/2in (7cm). Mint condition: **$10-25**. Pooh is standing outside of his door wearing a white nightcap and holding a candle. 2in (5cm). Mint condition: **$15-30**.

197. *Left:* Boots (England), circa 1989. This Pooh bubble bath container is constructed of yellow plastic in the shape of Pooh who is sitting on a brown plastic base with a honey pot in his hands. 6-1/2in (17cm). Excellent condition: **$45-55**. *Right:* Cliro Perfumeries (England), circa unknown. The 4in (10cm) figural Pooh soap is found in a colorful box depicting Pooh, Eeyore, Tigger, Piglet, Roo, Rabbit, and Owl. Pooh is standing with one arm raised to his head. Near mint in box: **$45-50**.

198. *Left:* Charpente, circa 1993, around Valentine's Day. The glossy ceramic bank depicts Christopher Robin and Pooh sitting on a log holding a red heart. The base is inscribed with "A little boy and his bear will always be playing in that enchanted place." 7in (18cm). Mint condition: **$35-50**. *Right:* Charpente, circa 1993. Pooh, Piglet, Tigger, and Eeyore surround a stump that serves as a glossy ceramic bank. The base is inscribed with "A very useful thing to keep bits and pieces in for today or tomorrow". 3in (8cm). Mint condition: **$30-40**.

199. Sears, circa 1988-1989. These jointed, flocked vinyl figurines are part of a set (see page 82), and consist of: yellow and white Rabbit, burnt orange with black stripes Tigger, orange Roo wearing a blue cotton shirt, and orange Kanga with a pink belly. Sizes range from 3in (8cm) to 5in (13cm) in height. Mint condition: **$20-25** each. Very good condition: **$8-15** each.

200. Sango, circa 1994. This ceramic five piece plate set features Pooh eating honey, Eeyore chewing on thistle, Piglet blowing a dandelion, Kanga and Roo bouncing, and bees and a blue balloon gliding above two honey pots. These were sold as a set through Tokyo Disneyland. 3-1/2in (9cm). Mint condition in original box: **$65-80**.

CHAPTER 5

TOYS AND MISCELLANEA

201. Sears, circa 1973. The vinyl case of the Winnie the Pooh play set unfolds into a house. Colorful cardboard characters and furniture stand on plastic holding disks. The upper section of the case depicts an outdoor scene. All of the major Pooh characters are included, even Gopher. Near mint condition: **$60-85**.

202. Chad Valley, circa mid-1960s. "Winnie the Pooh Give A Show" projector and slide set includes 112 color slides for 16 complete stories along with a plastic projector. Excellent condition in original box: **$125-175**.

203. Colorforms, circa early 1970s. Create your own adventures with this set of thin vinyl figures of Pooh, Christopher Robin, Piglet, Kanga and Roo, Tigger, Eeyore, Rabbit, and Owl that can be pressed onto a colorful scene. The figures are easily removable to change stories. Figures of bees, flowers, balloons, and honey pots are also included. Excellent condition in original box: **$65-80**.

204. Stephen Slesinger Inc., circa 1930. E.H. Shepard drawings of the Pooh characters are illustrated on a wooden tray. Black and white silhouettes form the border around the pastel-colored center and corner pictures. The tray is yellow with black trim. 17in (43cm) x 10-1/2in (27cm). Excellent condition: **$300-375.**

205. E. P. Dutton & Co., Inc., circa 1957. This set of 8 watercolor illustrations by E. H. Shepard is shown in its original box. All of the pictures are directly from "The World of Pooh" or "The World of Christopher Robin". 11in (28cm) x 14in (36cm). Mint condition in original box: **$45-75.**

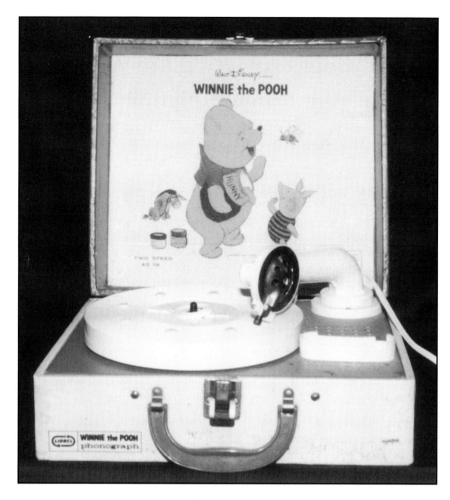

206. The Lionel Toy Corporation, circa 1964. Pooh, Piglet, and Eeyore are pictured on the outside and inside of this phonograph case. The designs of the pictures are indicative of the style used by Disney when they first obtained the copyright for Pooh (1964). The phonograph plays 45 and 78 speed records. Very good condition: **$100-150**.

207. American Telecommunications Corporation, circa 1976. A working telephone (not a toy) featuring a large plastic Pooh who is standing on a red and brown plastic base, holding the receiver in one hand and a blue butterfly (missing in photo) in the other. The phone was available as either a touchtone or rotary dial. Excellent condition: **$175-250**. Near mint condition with butterfly: **$300-400**.

208. Louis Marx Co., Inc., circa 1972-1974. A gold and red figural Pooh forms a child-size riding toy. A honey pot sits under Pooh's nose. 18in (46cm) x 15in (38cm). Excellent condition: **$75-100**.

209. *Bottom:* Sears, circa 1982-1985. Wooden Pooh cut-outs form the two long sides of this wooden toy wagon. Pooh is brown with a red shirt. 15in (38cm) long. Excellent condition: **$50-60**. *Top:* Sears, circa 1978-80. Vinyl clutch balls feature Pooh and Tigger in relief. One type of ball was sold in a gift set to baby and features a solid orange Tigger. Another type of ball depicts an orange Tigger with a white belly. Both balls picture a yellow Pooh with red shirt. 4-1/2in (11cm) diameter. Excellent condition: **$20-30**.

210. Sears, circa late 1970s-early 1980s. Records can be kept in these vinyl-coated cardboard boxes. The large box holds 33-1/3 records, while the small box holds 45s. The fronts and backs of the boxes have different scenes of Tigger and Pooh, but the small box is identical to the large box except for the size. Excellent condition: **$35-45** each.

211. *Left:* Ohio Art, circa 1976-1985. A paper Pooh is suspended in the center of the spinning top with pictures of Eeyore, Tigger, Piglet, and Pooh on the inside of the metal base. Plastic balls are held inside the clear plastic casing, and revolve when the top is spun. Excellent condition: **$35-55**. *Right:* Chein Playthings, circa 1972-1974. This uncommon metal and plastic spinning top has plastic-covered paper figures of Pooh, Tigger, and Eeyore suspended above a path. When the top spins, the characters appear to run along the path. Excellent condition: **$50-70**.

212. Meritus Industries, circa 1987-1989. This Pooh jack-in-the-box has a hard plastic box and a hard vinyl Pooh head that pops out of the box. The box plays "Pop Goes the Weasel". The decorative paper Pooh scenes on the sides of the box are glued to the out-side of the box. This toy was sold through Sears. Near mint condition: **$25-35**.

213. *Left and center:* Kohner Brothers Inc., circa 1965. At least two versions of the Pooh "Tricky Trapeze" were manufactured by Kohner Brothers Inc. around this time. The earlier version Pooh (style #4900, left) has jointed arms and fused legs. The later version (style #4995, center) has jointed arms and legs. The two yellow and red plastic Poohs appear slightly different as well. Both are connected from their arms to the plastic platform with string. They can spin and somersault by the push of the two white buttons on each side of the green plastic base. 5-1/2in (14cm). Excellent condition **$45-55**. *Right:* Kohner Brothers Inc., circa mid 1960s. The "mini-puppet" Pooh bends at every joint by the push of the button underneath the pink plastic base. The yellow and red plastic Pooh is multi-jointed and held together with string. Pushing the button in different places stresses different strings which results in a variety of possible movements by Pooh. 2in (5cm). Excellent condition: **$45-55**.

214. Marx, circa 1976-1977, Winnie-the-Pooh kazoo megaphone amplifies your voice. It was sold through Sears, and is constructed of red and white hard plastic with a yellow Pooh head mounted on top. 5-1/2in (14cm). Excellent condition: **$15-25**.

215. Multi-Print Milano (Italy), circa unknown. Their larger set of rubber ink stamps include: Pooh in two poses, Christopher Robin, Tigger with a mane, Kanga and Roo, Piglet, Rabbit with honey pot, Gopher with hard hat, Eeyore, Owl, Roo alone, and Pooh's house. The mane on Tigger is typical of Pooh products from Italy during this time. Also included is an ink pad and notebook. Box is 12-1/2in (32cm) x 8-1/2in (22cm). Very good condition in original box: **$45-60**.

216. *Left:* Gabriel Industries, circa 1975-1978. The plastic piano-shaped jack-in-the-box plays "This Old Man" when cranked. A hard plastic Pooh pops out of the top of the piano at the end of the song. The metal music mechanism is visible through a plastic window in the front of the piano. The keys of the piano are paper, glued to the plastic case, and do not move. This toy was sold through Sears. Excellent condition: **$35-55**. *Right:* Mattel (sold through Sears), circa 1971-1978. A paper Pooh scene is glued to the plastic case of this toy guitar. The wind-up mechanism plays "The Bear Went Over the Mountain". Very good condition: **$30-45**.

217. *Left:* Carnival, circa 1972, 1980-1982. This musical Pooh jack-in-the-box has a colorful metal case and octagonal lid. Each side of the box is illustrated with a variety of Pooh characters and some of the words to the "Winnie the Pooh" theme song. This song is played by the box when it is cranked, and Pooh pops out at the end of the song. Pooh is constructed of a hard plastic head with an unstuffed cloth body. The box was sold through Sears. Excellent condition: **$45-75**. *Center:* Sears, circa 1974-1976. This Winnie the Pooh musical jack-in-the-box plays "For He's the Jolly Good Fellow". The metal case shows different scenes of Pooh on each side. The Pooh inside the box has a hard plastic head and a yellow and orange cloth body. Excellent condition: **$45-60**. *Right:* Mattel, circa 1978. This musical box is the same as the 1976 box, except that the case is plastic with paper scenes glued to the sides. The box was sold through Sears. Excellent condition: **$30-40**.

218. Nabisco, Inc., circa 1973. This Winnie-the-Pooh Great Honey Crunchers rice cereal box featured an offer to receive "stock" in the "Honeypot Company". For one dollar, the buyer would receive a Pooh mask, two posters, a map of 100 Acre Woods, a puzzle, four postcards, a growth chart, placemat, stockholder's card, and stock certificate, all featuring the Pooh characters. In the box was one of eight credit cards which are described below. Original cereal box without "Honeypot Company" accessories in excellent condition: **$100-125.**

219. Nabisco, Inc., circa 1973. This Winnie-the-Pooh Great Honey Crunchers wheat cereal box featured a different pose of Pooh on its cover. This box offered a Pooh racing game by cutting out pieces on the back of the box and using "crazy car" provided within the box. Original cereal box in excellent condition: **$100-125**.

220. *Left:* Sears, circa 1988. This musical toy television has a flicker screen that makes characters appear to move as the inner scroll revolves. The toy plays "It's a Small World" when wound. A small toy clock is in the upper right corner. 9-1/2in (24cm) long. Mint condition in original box: **$35-50**. *Right:* Sears, circa 1971-1980. This older musical toy television was made by Fisher-Price, and features Pooh scenes that revolve while the "Winnie the Pooh" theme song is played. It has a plastic gold case and wind-up mechanism. 9in (23cm) x 10in (25cm). Excellent condition: **$35-50**.

221. *Left:* Meritus Industries, circa 1982-1985. This plastic Pooh crib toy can be mounted on the edge of the crib. When wound, it plays "Brahm's Lullaby" as the bee on Pooh's back moves, and Pooh travels down the edge of the crib. This commonly found toy was sold through Sears. 7in (18cm) x 8in (20cm). Excellent condition: **$15-20**. *Center:* Shelcore, circa 1988. When the string is pulled, this crib toy plays "London Bridge", while Pooh's arms move up and down. Pooh holds a plastic spoon coated with honey. The toy was sold through Sears. Mint condition: **$25**. *Right:* Sears, circa 1976-1983. When the string is pulled on this common crib toy, the "Winnie the Pooh" theme song plays, while Pooh's arms and eyes move up and down. 5-1/2in (14cm). Excellent condition: **$15-20**.

222. Mattel, Inc., circa 1978-1980. Winnie-the-Pooh See 'N Say hard plastic yellow phone allows you to dial your favorite Pooh character then pull the string to hear the message. This was sold through Sears. 9-1/2in (24cm) x 7-1/2in (19cm). Excellent condition, working: **$85-100**. Excellent condition, mute: **$30**.

223. Sears, circa 1988-1989. The gold plastic "Pooh Chorus" has piano-like keys along the front and vinyl Pooh heads mounted on colored bases on the top. When pushed, each key activates a same-colored Pooh to "sing" (a bell-like note is played and the appropriate Pooh opens his mouth.). Near mint condition: **$45-50**.

224. Multi-Print Milano (Italy), circa unknown. Their smaller set of ink stamps include: Tigger with a black mane, Pooh, Kanga and Roo, Rabbit with honey pot, Owl, Christopher Robin, and Eeyore. These same stamps comprise part of the larger set described above. The mane on Tigger is typical of Pooh products from Italy during this time. Also included is an ink pad and notebook. Box is 9-1/2in (24cm) x 6-3/4in (17cm). Very good condition in the original box: **$35-45**.

225. Sears, circa 1988-1989. The 100 Acre Woods train set includes: a two-piece brown plastic train; orange plastic track; a bridge; a plastic ferris wheel; a spinning teacup ride; a two horse carousel; and seven Pooh characters. The characters include: Pooh, Tigger, Eeyore, Piglet, Rabbit, Owl, and Kanga. The characters can ride each of the rides or drive the train. The rides are activated when the train stops at that ride. Excellent condition, complete: **$75-100**.

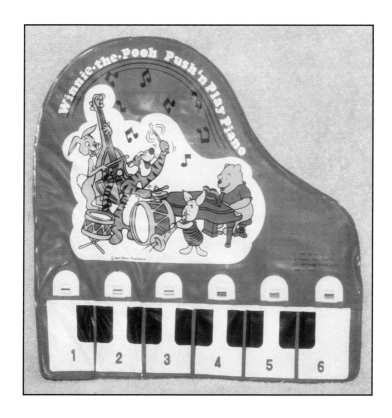

226. Shelcore, circa 1980. Rabbit, Tigger, Piglet, and Pooh are pictured as musicians on this soft vinyl toy piano. Sounds are heard when the keys are pressed. 13in (33cm) x 12in (31cm). Very good condition: **$15-25**.

227. Sears, circa 1982. The musical toy television contains scenes on a paper scroll that revolves while the "Winnie the Pooh" theme song plays. A flicker screen provides more animation to the characters as they revolve. The case is constructed of plastic. 10in (25cm) long. Excellent condition: **$33-50**.

228. Sears, circa 1980. A 100 Acre Woods scene covers this record player case, that is constructed of paper-covered chipboard. The record player includes a removable vinyl Pooh finger puppet. 12in (31cm) x 15in (38cm). Excellent condition: **$60-80**.

229. Sears, circa 1976-1977. Illustrations of Pooh and Tigger are pictured on the inside and on the outer side of this record player. The case is constructed of white plastic. The phonograph plays 45 and 33-1/3 speed records. 13in (33cm) x 12in (31cm). Excellent condition: **$45-60**.

230. Sears, circa 1980-1982. This record player can be found with either "Disco Pooh" (1980) or "Dancin' Pooh" (1982) printed on the front plastic panel. The case is constructed of chipboard covered with blue paper surrounding top and front plastic panels. Three colored blinking lights are housed under the plastic panels, and flash while records are playing. The player will play 45 and 33-1/3 speed records. The base is 12in (31cm) x 14in (36cm) while the top is 4in (10cm) shorter. Excellent condition: **$50-70**.

231. Sears, circa 1978. A Pooh cake can be baked in this aluminum cake pan. The bronze-colored exterior is accented with painted facial features to appear more decorative when hung on a wall. Two versions can be found. While Pooh is similar in either version, in one type, he is holding a honey pot; in the other type, he is not. 15in (38cm) x 10in (25cm). Excellent condition: **$40-50**.

232. *Left:* Durham Industries Inc., circa 1976-1977. The face of the plastic toy watch pictures Pooh walking with a honey pot in his hand. A bee is pictured on top of the honey pot. Two larger bees are on plastic disks at the 5:00 and 7:00 positions. When the watch is wound, the bees jiggle as the watch ticks. The case is yellow and the plastic band is red. Excellent condition: **$20-35**. *Right:* Lanar, circa 1975-1982. The face of this plastic toy watch features Pooh without a honey pot. The case is red and the band is yellow. Like the earlier version, two bees near Pooh's feet jiggle, and the watch ticks, when the watch is wound. Both watches are toys and do not keep time. Excellent condition: **$20-35**.

233. *Above:* Sears, circa 1988. This plastic shapefitter truck is equipped with soft vinyl figures of: Kanga with Roo in Pocket; Tigger; Piglet; Rabbit; and Eeyore. Pooh drives the truck and he bobs from side to side when the truck is pulled. Mint condition: **$35-45**. *Below:* Sears, circa 1978-1985. An older plastic shapefitter truck driven by Pooh who bobs from side to side when the truck is pulled. Tigger, Eeyore, Kanga, Roo, Piglet, and Owl are hard plastic figures mounted on differently shaped bases. They challenge the child to match shapes by placing each character in the appropriate spot in the truck. Excellent condition: **$35-45**.

234. Ideal Toy Corp., circa 1966. The Pooh "Whirl-A-Tune" is constructed of a vinyl Pooh head (complete with a bee) mounted atop a music box on a stick. Yellow pieces of felt hang down around the stick. When the handle is spun, the felt pieces fly outward, and "Parade of the Wooden Soldiers" is played. Near mint condition in original box: **$85-100**. Excellent condition, no box: **$50-70**.

235. *Left:* Chein, circa 1964. a tin-litho toy drum decorated with older Disney-style drawings of Eeyore, Piglet, Rabbit, Pooh, Owl, Roo, and Kanga. The drum is made completely of tin. 6in (15cm) diameter. Excellent condition: **$75-95**. *Right:* Tre-Jur, circa 1964. Confetti soap and a bath sponge are contained in this white and pink cardboard drum. Pooh is pictured on the lid and along the sides. The drum includes one wooden drumstick. 4-1/2in (12cm) high. Excellent condition: **$40-50**.

236. Aladdin Industries, circa late 1960s-1970s. Colorful different Pooh scenes decorate each outer panel of the metal lunchbox. When initially released, this box included a metal thermos (not shown). Beginning in 1974, a plastic thermos (pictured above) accompanied the box. Pooh scenes are also pictured on each type of thermos. Very good condition: **$150-175**. Thermos alone, very good condition: **$18-25**.

237. Sears, circa 1977-1983. The Winnie the Pooh talking toy phone allows the user to dial the picture of the character they wish to call. In the picture is a number to dial to hear that character. When the number is pressed, the character speaks. Eeyore says "I'm Eeyore. I'm sad.". Piglet says "I'm Piglet looking for Pooh.". Rabbit says, "Hello, I'm Rabbit." Kanga says, "I'm Kanga, and this is Roo". Owl says, "I'm Owl. Who are you?". Pooh says, "I'm Pooh. Good day to you.". The phone is constructed of white and red plastic, and is battery operated. Excellent condition: **$100-125**. Mute **$35**.

238. Sears, circa 1980-1982. This 54 piece service for six toy dish set (representative pieces shown) includes: plates picturing Pooh flipping pancakes; mugs picturing Pooh eating honey; yellow goblets; knives; forks; spoons; napkins; cooking utensils; one tray picturing Tigger, Eeyore, and Pooh; one coffee pot with cover (Pooh eating honey is pictured on the pot); two Windsor sauce pans and one pan with a cover (Pooh, Tigger, and Eeyore are pictured on the pans). The pans and coffee pot are aluminum, while most of the other pieces are plastic. Very good condition: **$30-45**.

239. Nabisco, Inc., circa 1973. Good Deed credit cards were premiums in the cereal described above. Each card featured one Pooh character and allowed the holder to a benefit such as a favorite meal in exchange for completing a task such as finishing homework. Excellent condition: **$10** each.

240. Sears, circa 1972. The "Pooh Junior Artist Set" is manufactured by General Mills Fun Group Inc., and includes: 5 different colored paints, a paint brush, 14 Pooh and friends pictures to paint, and a colorful plastic bib. Mint in original box: **$45-60**.

241. *Left:* Sears, circa 1977-1980. Pull the string and Pooh's arms throw the small colored balls inside the plastic window of the crib toy. Push the yellow button, and the toy squeaks. Very good condition: **$35-40**. *Right:* Walt Disney Productions, circa 1972-1975. The "Pooh and Honey Pot" game features Pooh sitting at the door of his plastic tree house holding a honey pot. Several other honey pots line the front, and when pushed, opens doors to reveal the other Pooh characters. One honey pot button activates Pooh to move his pot to his face and back, while another lifts Tigger from the tree with a "click" noise. Owl is lifted from the other side of the tree with a "tweet" noise, while Kanga, Roo, and Piglet throw open their shutters and make "squeak" and "squawk" noises. 8in (20cm) high. Very good condition: **$50-65**.

242. Sears, circa 1970-1975. A pull ring activates the plastic toy clock that plays the Winnie the Pooh theme song, while a plastic bird moves in and out and the hands of clock rotate. This item was sold through Sears. 9-1/2in (24cm) x 11in (28cm). Very good condition: **$25-35**.

243. Sears, circa 1975-1978. The "Bee 'N Hunny" game is a plastic toy pinball machine. A ball with a bee pictured on it, gets kicked and thrown from Pooh to Piglet to Owl to Tigger then into the hive at the top. When this sequence is successful, a honey pot falls to the bottom. Bells ring when each button is pushed. 10-1/2in (26cm). Near mint condition: **$50-70**.

244. Arco, circa 1985. The Winnie-the-Pooh bath time boat contains a soft vinyl Tigger squirt gun, a hard plastic Pooh with sponge on bottom, and a hard plastic Eeyore figurine that sits in a sieve. 11in (28cm). Sold through Sears. An earlier version was sold through Sears in the early 1980s. The earlier version had a white boat and an Eeyore whose upper body was fused to the sieve. Excellent condition: **$25-35**.

245. *Left:* Shelcore Inc, circa 1983-1985. The chiming roly poly yellow plastic Pooh has a plastic mirror in his belly. This toy was sold through Sears. 8in (20cm) tall. Excellent condition: **$20-35.** *Center:* Arco, circa 1981-1982. This hard plastic chiming roly poly Pooh is yellow with a red "shirt", and balances a brown honey pot on his nose. His arms are jointed. The toy was sold through Sears. Excellent condition: **$45-55**. *Right:* Gabriel Industries Inc, circa 1976-1977. The chiming roly poly yellow and red Pooh sits in a brown tub filled with "water". The toy is plastic with a weighted bottom, and was sold through Sears. 8in (20cm) tall. Excellent condition: **$40-50**.

118

246. *Above:* Kohner, circa 1973-1977. When this yellow plastic car driven by Pooh is pulled, Pooh's head moves as he steers. The toy was sold through Sears. 10in (25cm) long, 8in (20cm) tall. Excellent condition: **$55-75**. *Right:* Sears, circa 1988. The Pooh red plastic toy musical radio plays Braham's Lullaby while Pooh's head moves. This toy was recalled by Sears shortly after its introduction. A nearly duplicate toy was later seen on the market called "Bear radio". 5-1/2in (14cm). Excellent condition: **$25-35**.

ABOUT THE AUTHOR

Carol lives in Washington State with her husband and two young boys. She has a doctorate degree in Zoology and works as a Fish Biologist for the Washington Department of Fish and Wildlife. Her interest in Pooh items began as a child, when The World of Pooh was given to her by her parents, and has continued when extra time has allowed. She is most grateful for the wonderful friends she has met while pursuing this hobby. Other interests include water sports, gardening, and raising dalmatians.